"A brilliant show."—*Cue*

"Fascinating"—*New Yorker*

"Great"—*Newsweek*

On March 15, 1956 one of the great romances of all time began. That was the night MY FAIR LADY opened at the Mark Hellinger Theatre in New York, and Eliza Doolittle and Henry Higgins waltzed away with the affection of the U. S. A.

Audiences applauded. Critics cheered. And theatre history was made.

Later this smash Broadway hit was made into a loverly motion picture, starring Audrey Hepburn and Rex Harrison—a motion picture that delighted audiences all across the country.

This beautiful Signet edition recaptures in words and lyrics all the magic of a love story that is loved around the world.

World Drama from SIGNET CLASSIC

MY FAIR LADY

A Musical Play in Two Acts

Based on *Pygmalion* by Bernard Shaw

Adaptation and Lyrics by
ALAN JAY LERNER

Music by
FREDERICK LOEWE

A SIGNET BOOK

NEW AMERICAN LIBRARY

SIGNET, SIGNET CLASSIC, MENTOR, PLUME, MERIDIAN AND NAL
BOOKS *are published by New American Library,
1633 Broadway, New York, New York 10019*

FIRST PRINTING, JULY, 1958

18   19   20   21   22   23   24   25   26

PRINTED IN CANADA

FOR NANCY,
WITH LOVE

Note

For the published version of *Pygmalion*, Shaw wrote a preface and an epilogue which he called a sequel. I have omitted the preface because the information contained therein is less pertinent to *My Fair Lady* than it is to *Pygmalion*.

I have omitted the sequel because in it Shaw explains how Eliza ends not with Higgins but with Freddy and—Shaw and Heaven forgive me!—I am not certain he is right.

A. J. L.

My Fair Lady opened in New York March 15, 1956, at the Mark Hellinger Theatre with the following cast:

(In order of appearance)

Buskers	Imelda de Martin
	Carl Jeffrey
	Joe Rocco
Mrs. Eynsford-Hill	Viola Roache
Eliza Doolittle	Julie Andrews
Freddy Eynsford-Hill	Michael King
Colonel Pickering	Robert Coote
A Bystander	Christopher Hewett
Henry Higgins	Rex Harrison
Selsey Man	Gordon Dilworth
Hoxton Man	David Thomas
Another Bystander	Rod McLennan
First Cockney	Reid Shelton
Second Cockney	Glenn Kezer
Third Cockney	James Morris
Fourth Cockney	Herb Surface
Bartender	David Thomas
Harry	Gordon Dilworth
Jamie	Rod McLennan
Alfred P. Doolittle	Stanley Holloway
Mrs. Pearce	Philippa Bevans
Mrs. Hopkins	Olive Reeves-Smith
Butler	Reid Shelton
Servants	Rosemary Gaines
	Colleen O'Connor
	Muriel Shaw

	Gloria van Dorpe
	Glenn Kezer
Mrs. Higgins	Cathleen Nesbitt
Chauffeur	Barton Mumaw
Footmen	Gordon Ewing
	William Krach
Lord Boxington	Gordon Dilworth
Lady Boxington	Olive Reeves-Smith
Constable	Barton Mumaw
Flower Girl	Cathy Conklin
Zoltan Karpathy	Christopher Hewett
Flunkey	Paul Brown
Queen of Transylvania	Maribel Hammer
Ambassador	Rod McLennan
Bartender	Paul Brown
Mrs. Higgins' Maid	Judith Williams
Singing Ensemble	Melisande Congdon
	Lola Fisher
	Rosemary Gaines
	Maribel Hammer
	Colleen O'Connor
	Muriel Shaw
	Patti Spangler
	Gloria van Dorpe
	Paul Brown
	Gordon Ewing
	Glenn Kezer
	William Krach
	James Morris
	Reid Shelton
	Herb Surface
	David Thomas

Dancing Ensemble	Estelle Aza
	Cathy Conklin
	Margaret Cuddy
	Imelda de Martin
	Pat Diamond
	Pat Drylie
	Barbara Heath
	Vera Lee
	Nancy Lynch
	Judith Williams
	Thatcher Clarke
	Crandall Diehl
	David Evans
	Carl Jeffrey
	Barton Mumaw
	Gene Nettles
	Paul Olson
	Joe Rocco
	Fernando Schaffenburg
	James White

My Fair Lady was produced by Herman Levin
  Directed by Moss Hart
  Scenery by Oliver Smith
  Costumes by Cecil Beaton
  Choreography by Hanya Holm
  Lighting by Feder
  Orchestra conducted by Franz Allers
  Orchestrations by Robert Russell Bennet and Phil Lang

Musical Synopsis

Act One

1. Street Entertainers	THE 3 BUSKERS
2. "Why Can't the English?"	HIGGINS
3. "Wouldn't It Be Loverly?"	ELIZA and COSTERMONGERS
4. "With A Little Bit of Luck"	DOOLITTLE, HARRY and JAMIE
5. "I'm An Ordinary Man"	HIGGINS
6. "With A Little Bit of Luck" (Reprise)	DOOLITTLE and FRIENDS
7. "Just You Wait"	ELIZA
8. "The Rain in Spain"	HIGGINS, ELIZA and PICKERING
9. "I Could Have Danced All Night"	ELIZA, MRS. PEARCE and MAIDS
10. Ascot Gavotte	SPECTATORS AT THE RACE
11. "On the Street Where You Live"	FREDDY
12. "The Embassy Waltz"	HIGGINS, ELIZA, KARPATHY and GUESTS

Act Two

1. "You Did It"	HIGGINS, PICKERING, MRS. PEARCE and SERVANTS
2. "Just You Wait" (Reprise)	ELIZA
3. "On the Street Where You Live" (Reprise)	FREDDY

Act One

The place is London, the time 1912.

Scene *1:* Outside the Royal Opera House, Covent Garden. A cold March night.

Scene *2:* Tenement section—Tottenham Court Road. Immediately following.

Scene *3:* Higgins' study. The following morning.

Scene *4:* Tenement section—Tottenham Court Road. Three days later.

Scene *5:* Higgins' study. Later that day.

Scene *6:* Near the race meeting, Ascot. A July afternoon.

Scene *7:* Inside a club tent, Ascot. Immediately following.

Scene *8:* Outside Higgins' house, Wimpole Street. Later that afternoon.

Scene *9:* Higgins' study. Six weeks later.

Scene *10:* The promenade of the Embassy. Later that night.

Scene *11:* The ballroom of the Embassy. Immediately following.

Act Two

ACT ONE

Scene I

Outside the Royal Opera House, Covent Garden.

TIME: After theater, a cold March night.

AT RISE: *The opera is just over. Richly gowned, beautifully tailored Londoners are pouring from the Opera House and making their way across Covent Garden in search of taxis. Some huddle together under the columns of St. Paul's Church which are partially in view on one side of the stage. On the opposite side, there is a smudge-pot fire around which a quartet of costermongers are warming themselves. Calls of "Taxi" punctuate the icy air.*

THREE STREET ENTERTAINERS, BUSKERS, *rush on to perform a few acrobatic tricks, stunts, and dance steps. They detain the crowd for a moment. The female member of the trio passes the hat as her two associates continue and reach the "climax" of their act.*

MRS. EYNSFORD-HILL, *a middle-aged lady in evening dress and her son* FREDDY, *a young man of twenty, also in evening dress, come through the crowd in search of a taxi. One of the buskers collides into him. He is thrown backwards and strikes a figure hidden behind a group of people who now come flying forward and lands in a heap. She is a flower girl,* ELIZA DOOLITTLE. *Her basket of flowers has been knocked from her hands and her violets scattered about. She is not at all an attractive person. She is perhaps eighteen, perhaps twenty,*

15

*hardly older. She wears a little sailor hat of
black straw that has long been exposed to the
dust and soot of London and has seldom if
ever been brushed. Her hair needs washing
rather badly; its mousy color can hardly be
natural. She wears a shoddy shawl, a dirty
blouse with a coarse apron. Her boots are
much the worse for wear. She is no doubt as
clean as she can afford to be; but compared to
the ladies she is very dirty. Her features are no
worse than theirs; but their condition leaves
something to be desired, and she needs the
services of a dentist.*

ELIZA
Aaaooowww!

FREDDY
(*Clumsily trying to help her*) I'm frightfully sorry.

ELIZA
(*Wailing*) Two bunches of violets trod in the mud! A
full day's wages. Why don't you look where you're going?

MRS. EYNSFORD-HILL
Get a taxi, Freddy. Do you want me to catch pneumonia?

FREDDY
I'm sorry, mother. I'll get a taxi right away. (*To* ELIZA)
Sorry. (*He goes*)
        (COLONEL PICKERING *emerges dressed in evening
        clothes and looking for a taxi. He is a middle-aged
        gentleman of the amiable military type*)

ELIZA
(*To* MRS. EYNSFORD-HILL) Oh, he's your son, is he?
Well, if you'd done your duty by him as a mother should,
you wouldn't let him spoil a poor girl's flowers and then
run away without paying.

MRS. EYNSFORD-HILL
Go on about your business, my girl. (*She follows her
son*)

ELIZA
(*Muttering to herself, as she collects her flowers*) Two
bunches of violets trod in the mud.

PICKERING

(*Calling off*) Taxi! Taxi!

ELIZA

(*To* PICKERING) I say, Captain, buy a flower off a poor girl.

PICKERING

I'm sorry. I haven't any change.

ELIZA

I can change half a crown. Here, take this for tuppence.

PICKERING

(*Trying his pockets*) I really haven't any—stop: here's three ha'pence, if that's any use to you.

ELIZA

(*Disappointed, but thinking three halfpence better than nothing*) Thank you, sir.

A BYSTANDER

(*To* ELIZA) Here, you be careful. Better give him a flower fer it. There's a bloke there behind the pillar taking down every blessed word you're saying.

(*The* CROWD *turns to look behind the pillar*)

ELIZA

(*Springing up terrified*) I ain't done nothin' wrong by speakin' to the gentleman! I've a right to sell flowers if I keep off the kerb. I'm a respectable girl; so help me, I never spoke to him except to ask him to buy a flower off me.

(*There is a general hubbub, mostly sympathetic to* ELIZA, *but deprecating her excessive sensibility*)

ANOTHER BYSTANDER

What's the row?

A HOXTON MAN

What's all the bloomin' noise?

A SELSEY MAN

There's a tec takin' her down.

ELIZA

(*Crying wildly—to* PICKERING) Oh, sir, don't let him charge me! You dunno what it means to me. They'll take

away my character and drive me on the streets for
speakin' to gentlemen.

> (PROFESSOR HIGGINS *pivots around the post and
> into view*)

HIGGINS

There! There! There! Who's hurting you, you silly
girl! What do you take me for?

ELIZA

(*To* HIGGINS—*still hysterical*) On my Bible oath, I never
said a word. . . .

HIGGINS

(*Overbearing, but good-humored*) Oh, shut up, shut
up. Do I look like a policeman?

ELIZA

Then what did you take down my words for? How do I
know whether you took me down right? You just show
me what you wrote about me.

> (HIGGINS *opens his book and holds it steadily under
> her nose, though the pressure of the mob trying to
> read it over his shoulders would upset a weaker
> man*)

What's this? That ain't proper writing. I can't read that.

HIGGINS

I can. (*Reads, reproducing her pronunciation*) I say,
Captain, buy a flower off a poor girl.

ELIZA

It's because I called him Captain! I meant no harm. (*To*
PICKERING) Oh, sir, don't let him lay a charge agen me
for a word like that. You . . .

PICKERING

Charge! I make no charge. (*To* HIGGINS) Really, sir, if
you are a detective, you need not begin protecting me
against molestation by young women until I ask you.
Anybody could see the girl meant no harm.

THE SELSEY MAN

He ain't a tec. He's a gentleman. Look at his shoes.

HIGGINS

(*Turning on him genially*) And how are all your people
down at Selsey?

THE SELSEY MAN
(*Suspiciously*) Who told you my people come from Selsey?

HIGGINS
Never mind. They did. (*To* ELIZA) How do you come to be up so far east? You were born in Lisson Grove.

ELIZA
(*Appalled*) Ooooh, what harm is there in my leaving Lisson Grove? It wasn't fit for a pig to live in; and I had to pay four-and-six a week. Oh, boo-hoo-oo—

HIGGINS
Live where you like; but stop that noise. (*With pad in hand, he becomes interested in the accents of the men grouped around the fire*)

PICKERING
(*To* ELIZA) Come, come! He can't touch you; you have a right to live where you please.

ELIZA
(*Subsiding into a brooding melancholy and talking very low-spiritedly to herself*) I'm a good girl, I am.

THE HOXTON MAN
Do you know where *I* come from?

HIGGINS
(*Promptly*) Hoxton.

THE HOXTON MAN
(*Amazed*) Well, who said I didn't! Blimey, you know everything, you do.
(*Titterings. Popular interest in the note-taker's performance increases*)

ANOTHER BYSTANDER
(*Indicating* PICKERING) Tell him where he comes from, if you want to go fortunetelling.

HIGGINS
Cheltenham, Harrow, Cambridge and India.

PICKERING
Quite right.

AND STILL ANOTHER BYSTANDER
Blimey, he ain't a tec; he's a bloomin' busybody, that's what he is!
(*The crowd starts leaving, highly impressed*)

PICKERING
May I ask, sir, do you do this sort of thing for a living on the music halls?
(*All have gone except the four* COSTERMONGERS *grouped about the smudge-pot fire,* HIGGINS, PICKERING, *and* ELIZA, *who is seated on the kerb against one of the pillars arranging her flowers and pitying herself in murmurs*)

HIGGINS
I have thought of that. Perhaps I will someday.

ELIZA
He's no gentleman, he ain't, to interfere with a poor girl.

PICKERING
How do you do it, if I may ask?

HIGGINS
Simple phonetics. The science of speech. That's my profession, also my hobby. Anyone can spot an Irishman or a Yorkshireman by his brogue. I can place a man within six miles; I can place him within two miles in London. (*Indicating* ELIZA) Sometimes within two streets.

ELIZA
Ought to be ashamed of himself, unmanly coward!

PICKERING
But is there a living in that?

HIGGINS
Oh, yes. Quite a fat one.

ELIZA
Let him mind his own business and leave a poor girl—

HIGGINS
(*Explosively*) Woman! Cease this detestable boohooing instantly or else seek the shelter of some other place of worship.

ELIZA

(*With feeble defiance*) I've a right to be here if I like, same as you.

HIGGINS

A woman who utters such depressing and disgusting sounds has no right to be anywhere—no right to live. Remember that you are a human being with a soul and the divine gift of articulate speech; that your native language is the language of Shakespeare and Milton and the Bible; and don't sit there crooning like a bilious pigeon.

ELIZA

(*Quite overwhelmed, looking up at him in mingled wonder and deprecation without daring to raise her head*) Aoooooooooooow!

HIGGINS

Look at her—a pris'ner of the gutters;
Condemned by ev'ry syllable she utters.
By right she should be taken out and hung
For the cold-blooded murder of the English tongue!

ELIZA

A-o-o-o-w!

HIGGINS

(*Imitating her*) Aoooow! Heavens, what a noise!

This is what the British population
Calls an element'ry education.

PICKERING

Come, sir, I think you picked a poor example.

HIGGINS

Did I?

Hear them down in Soho Square
Dropping aitches everywhere,
Speaking English any way they like. (*To one of the* COSTERMONGERS *at the fire*) You, sir, did you go to school?

COSTERMONGER

Whatya tike me fer, a fool?

HIGGINS

(*To* PICKERING)
No one taught him "take" instead of "tike."
Hear a Yorkshireman, or worse,
Hear a Cornishman converse.
I'd rather hear a choir singing flat.
Chickens cackling in a barn . . .
(*Pointing to* ELIZA)
Just like this one—!

ELIZA

—Garn!

HIGGINS

I ask you, sir, what sort of word is that?
It's "Aooow" and "Garn" that keep her in her place.
Not her wretched clothes and dirty face.

Why can't the English teach their children how to
speak?
This verbal class distinction by now should be antique.
If you spoke as she does, sir,
Instead of the way you do,
Why, you might be selling flowers, too.

PICKERING

I beg your pardon!

HIGGINS

An Englishman's way of speaking absolutely classifies
him
The moment he talks he makes some other English-
man despise him.
One common language I'm afraid we'll never get.
Oh, why can't the English learn to set
A good example to people whose English is painful to
your ears?
The Scotch and the Irish leave you close to tears.

There even are places where English completely disappears.
In America, they haven't used it for years!
Why can't the English teach their children how to
speak?

Norwegians learn Norwegian; the Greeks are taught
    their Greek.
In France every Frenchman knows his language from
    "A" to "Zed"
The French never care what they do, actually, as long
    as they pronounce it properly.

Arabians learn Arabian with the speed of summer
    lightning.
The Hebrews learn it backwards, which is absolutely
    frightening.
But use proper English, you're regarded as a freak.
Why can't the English,
Why can't the English learn to speak?

(*He looks thoughtfully at* ELIZA) You see this creature
with her kerbstone English; the English that will keep
her in the gutter to the end of her days? Well, sir, in six
months I could pass her off as a duchess at an Embassy
ball. I could even get her a place as a lady's maid or shop
assistant, which requires better English.

ELIZA

(*Rising with sudden interest*) Here, what's that you say?

HIGGINS

Yes, you squashed cabbage leaf, you disgrace to the
noble architecture of these columns, you incarnate insult
to the English language; I could pass you off as the
Queen of Sheba.

PICKERING

(*Interested in* HIGGINS *but more so in finding a taxi,
thinks he sees one and moves quickly to hail it*) Taxi!

ELIZA

Aooow! (*To* PICKERING) You don't believe that, Captain?

PICKERING

Taxi! (*He loses the cab and comes back*) Oh, well, anything is possible. I myself am a student of Indian dialects.

HIGGINS

(*Eagerly*) Are you? Do you know Colonel Pickering, the
author of *Spoken Sanskrit?*

PICKERING
I am Colonel Pickering. Who are you?

HIGGINS
Henry Higgins, author of *Higgins' Universal Alphabet*.

PICKERING
(*Amazed*) I came from India to meet you!

HIGGINS
(*With enthusiasm*) I was going to India to meet you!

PICKERING
(*Extending his hand*) Higgins!

HIGGINS
(*Extending his*) Pickering! (*They shake hands*) Where are you staying?

PICKERING
At the Carleton.

HIGGINS
No, you're not. You're staying at 27-A Wimpole Street. Come with me and we'll have a jaw over supper.

PICKERING
Right you are.
    (*They start off together*)

ELIZA
(*To* HIGGINS *as they pass her*) Buy a flower, kind sir. I'm short for my lodging.

HIGGINS
(*Shocked at the girl's mendacity*) Liar! You said you could change half a crown.

ELIZA
(*In desperation*) You ought to be stuffed with nails, you ought. Here! (*Shoving her basket at him*) Take the whole bloomin' basket for sixpence!
    (*The church clock strikes the second quarter*)

HIGGINS
(*He raises his hat solemnly*) Ah. The church. A reminder. (*Throws a handful of money into the basket and follows* PICKERING) Indian dialects have always fascinated me. I have records of over fifty.

PICKERING
　　Have you, now. Did you know there are over two hun-
　　dred?

HIGGINS
　　By George, it's worse than London. Do you know them
　　all?
　　　　(*They disappear down the street*)

ELIZA
　　(*Picking up a half crown*) Ah-ow-ooh! (*Picking up a
　　couple of florins*) Aaah-ow-ooh! (*Picking up several
　　coins*) Aaaaaaah-ow-ooh! (*Picking up a half sovereign*)
　　Aaaaaaaaaah-ow-ooh!! (*She skips to the fire to display
　　her wealth*)

FIRST COSTERMONGER
　　(*With a sweep of his hat*) Shouldn't you stand up, gen-
　　tlemen? We've got a bloomin' heiress in our midst!

SECOND COSTERMONGER
　　(*Rises and clicking heels*) Would you be lookin' for a
　　good butler, Eliza?

ELIZA
　　(*Haughtily*) You won't do. (*She walks away*)

SECOND COSTERMONGER
　　　　It's rather dull in town,
　　　　I think I'll take me to Paree.

THIRD COSTERMONGER
　　　　The missus wants to open up,
　　　　The castle in Capri!

FIRST COSTERMONGER
　　　　Me doctor recommends
　　　　A quiet summer by the sea.

THE FOUR
　　　　Mmmmmmmm! Mmmmmmm!
　　　　Wouldn't it be loverly!

THIRD COCKNEY
　　Where're ya bound for this spring, Eliza? Biarritz?

ELIZA
　　　　(*Leaning against the pillar*)

All I want is a room somewhere,
Far away from the cold night air;
With one enormous chair . . .
Oh, wouldn't it be loverly?

Lots of choc'late for me to eat;
Lots of coal makin' lots of heat;
Warm face, warm hands, warm feet . . . !
Oh, wouldn't it be loverly?

Oh, so loverly sittin' absobloominlutely still
I would never budge till spring
Crept over me winder sill.

Someone's head restin' on my knee,
Warm and tender as he can be,
Who takes good care of me . . .
Oh, wouldn't it be loverly?
Loverly! Loverly!
Loverly! Loverly!

(*As* ELIZA *spins out her daydream, a few other*
FLOWER GIRLS *and* VENDERS *are drawn on and
stand silently listening. When she finishes, the four
at the fire beguiled into the mood repeat the refrain
as* ELIZA *and the others act out a dinner in an ex-
pensive restaurant: the ordering, the wine, the food
—and riding home in a taxi afterwards. A dustcart
serves the purpose. An icy blast blows across the
market place bringing them quickly back to reality
and they all gather around the fire and warm their
hands*)

Scene 2

*Tenement section, Tottenham Court Road. A
shabby back alley filled with atmosphere for
everyone but those who live there. There is a
small public house on one side of the stage, a
converted mews on the other and, rising in the
end of the street that divides the two, the misty*

outline of St. Paul's Cathedral (Chris Wren's, not the Covent Garden St. Paul's)

TIME: *Later that evening.*

There is a commotion at the pub. GEORGE, *the bartender, is discovered forcibly evicting two disorderly members of the lowest possible class, by the name* HARRY *and* JAMIE. GEORGE *now directs his remarks into the bar.*

BARTENDER
I ain't runnin' no charity bazaar. Drinks is to be paid for or not drunk. Come on, Doolittle. Out you go. Hop it now, Doolittle. On the double. On the double.

(ALFRED DOOLITTLE *emerges. He is an elderly but vigorous dustman, clad in the costume of his profession, including a hat with a black brim covering his neck and shoulders. He has well marked and rather interesting features, and seems equally free from fear and conscience. He has a remarkably expressive voice, the result of a habit of giving vent to his feelings without reserve. His present pose is that of wounded honor and casual disdain*)

DOOLITTLE
Thanks for your hospitality, George. Send the bill to Buckingham Palace (*The* BARTENDER *exits into pub as* DOOLITTLE *joins his associates*) Hyde Park to walk through on a fine spring night; the whole ruddy city of London to roam about in sellin' her bloomin' flowers. I give her all that, and then I disappears and leaves her on her own to enjoy it. Now if that ain't worth half a crown now and again, I'll take off my belt and give her what for.

JAMIE
You got a good heart, Alfie, but if you want that half a crown from Eliza, you better have a good story to go with it.

(ELIZA *ambles on*)

DOOLITTLE
(*With paternal joy*) Eliza! What a surprise!

ELIZA
(*Walking past him*) Not a brass farthing.

DOOLITTLE

(*Grabbing her arm*) Now you look here, Eliza. You wouldn't have the heart to send me home to your step-mother without a bit of liquid protection, now would you?

ELIZA

Stepmother. Ha! Stepmother, indeed!

DOOLITTLE

Well, I'm willing to marry her. It's me that suffers by it. I'm a slave to that woman, Eliza. Just because I ain't her lawful husband. (*Lovably*) Come on, Eliza, slip your old Dad half a crown to go home on.

ELIZA

(*Taking a coin from her basket, flipping it in air and catching it*) Well, I had a bit of luck meself tonight. So here. (*Gives him coin*)

HARRY

(*Jubilantly calls into pub*) George! Three glorious beers!

ELIZA

But don't keep comin' around countin' on half crowns from me! (*She disappears into the converted mews*)

DOOLITTLE

Goodnight, Eliza! You're a noble daughter! (*He turns to his friends smugly*) You see, boys, I told you not to go home! It's just Faith, Hope and a little bit of luck!

The Lord above gave man an arm of iron
So he could do his job and never shirk.
The Lord above gave man an arm of iron—but
With a little bit of luck,
With a little bit of luck,
Someone else'll do the blinkin' work!

THE THREE

With a little bit . . . . with a little bit . . . .
With a little bit of luck
You'll never work!

DOOLITTLE

The Lord above made liquor for temptation,
To see if man could turn away from sin.

The Lord above made liquor for temptation—but
With a little bit of luck,
With a little bit of luck,
When temptation comes you'll give right in!

THE THREE

With a little bit .... with a little bit ....
With a little bit of luck,
You'll give right in.

DOOLITTLE

Oh, you can walk the straight and narrow;
But with a little bit of luck
You'll run amuck!

The gentle sex was made for man to marry,
To share his nest and see his food is cooked.
The gentle sex was made for man to marry—but
With a little bit of luck,
With a little bit of luck,
You can have it all and not get hooked.

THE THREE

With a little bit .... with a little bit ....
With a little bit of luck
You won't get hooked.
With a little bit .... with a little bit ....
With a little bit of bloomin' luck!
(*An* ANGRY WOMAN *pokes her head out of the up-stairs window of the mews*)

ANGRY WOMAN

Shut your face down there! How's a woman supposed to get her rest?

DOOLITTLE

I'm tryin' to keep 'em quiet, lady!
(*The voice of an* ANGRY MAN *is heard down the street*)

ANGRY MAN

Shut up! Once and for all, shut up!

ANOTHER ANGRY MAN

One more sound, so help me, I'll call a copper!

DOOLITTLE
Here, here, here! Stop that loud talk! People are tryin' to sleep! (*He turns to his friends*) Let's try to be neigh-borly-like, boys. After all. . .

(*Sings softly*)
The Lord above made man to help his neighbor,
No matter where, on land, or sea, or foam.
The Lord above made man to help his neighbor—but
With a little bit of luck,
With a little bit of luck,
When he comes around you won't be home!

JAMIE *and* HARRY
With a little bit . . . . with a little bit . . . .
With a little bit of luck,
You won't be home.

DOOLITTLE
They're always throwin' goodness at you;
But with a little bit of luck
A man can duck!

Oh, it's a crime for man to go philanderin'
And fill his wife's poor heart with grief and doubt.
Oh, it's a crime for man to go philanderin'—but
With a little bit of luck,
With a little bit of luck,
You can see the bloodhound don't find out!

THE THREE
(*At the top of their lungs*)
With a little bit . . . . with a little bit . . . .
With a little bit of luck
She won't find out!
With a little bit . . . . with a little bit . . . .
With a little bit of bloomin' luck!
(*Angry cries descend on them from all over the neighborhood. They cheerfully disregard them and re-enter the pub*)

Scene 3

HIGGINS' *study in Wimpole Street.*

It is a room on the first floor with one window in an alcove looking out on the street and double doors in the middle of the back wall. There is a balcony above them with stairs to one side leading up to it. There is another door on the balcony and the wall of the balcony is entirely covered with bookcases. Next to the door is a small table upon which is a recording machine and speaker horn.

There is a desk below the alcove upon which is a small bust of Plato, a mass of papers, several tuning forks of different sizes, and a telephone. Next to the desk is a small xylophone and another recorder and speaker. The alcove behind is a mass of filing cabinets and books. There is a bird cage containing a bird next to the window.

There is a sofa in the middle of the room, an easy chair next to the stairs and a small stool in front of the desk. Behind the easy chair is another recording machine and, against the wall by the double doors, still another.

TIME: *The next day.*

The room is dark. In the darkness between the scenes strange-guttural sounds pour forth from the public address system. PICKERING *is seated in the easy chair.* HIGGINS *is standing by the recording machine next to his desk. The strange sounds heard in the darkness a moment before are now discovered to be coming from the recorder. When the lights go on, as they will in a moment,* HIGGINS *in the morning light is seen to be a robust, vital, appetizing sort of man of forty or thereabouts. He is of the energetic*

*scientific type, heartily, even violently, inter-
ested in everything that can be studied as a
scientific subject, and careless about himself
and other people, including their feelings. He
is, in fact, but for his years and size, rather like
a very impetuous baby "taking notice" eagerly
and loudly, and requiring almost as much
watching to keep him out of unintended mischief. His manner varies from genial bullying
when he is in a good humor to stormy petulance
when anything goes wrong; but he is so entirely
frank and void of malice that he remains likable
even in his least reasonable moments.*

PICKERING
I say, Higgins, couldn't we turn on the lights?

HIGGINS
Nonsense, you hear much better in the dark.

PICKERING
But it's a fearful strain listening to all these vowel sounds.
I'm quite done up for this morning.
          (MRS. PEARCE *enters. She is* HIGGINS' *housekeeper*)

MRS. PEARCE
Mr. Higgins, are you there?

HIGGINS
What is it, Mrs. Pearce? (*He turns down the volume of
the machine*)

MRS. PEARCE
A young woman wants to see you, sir.

HIGGINS
(*Turning the machine off*) A young woman! What does
she want? (*He switches on the light*) Has she an interesting accent? (*To* PICKERING) Let's have her up. Show her
up, Mrs. Pearce.

MRS. PEARCE
Very well, sir. It's for you to say. (*She goes out into the
hall*)

HIGGINS
This is rather a bit of luck. I'll show you how I make rec-

ords. We'll set her talking; and I'll take her down in
Bell's Visible Speech; then in Broad Romic; and then
we'll get her on the phonograph so that you can turn her
on as often as you like with the written transcript before
you.

MRS. PEARCE

(*Returning*) This is the young woman, sir.

> (ELIZA *enters in state. She has a hat with three os-
> trich feathers, orange, sky-blue, and red. She has a
> nearly clean apron, and the shoddy coat has been
> tidied a little. The pathos of this deplorable figure,
> with its innocent vanity and consequential air,
> touches* PICKERING, *who has already straightened
> himself in the presence of* MRS. PEARCE. *But as to*
> HIGGINS, *the only distinction he makes between men
> and women is that when he is neither bullying nor
> exclaiming to the heavens against some feather-
> weight cross, he coaxes women as a child coaxes its
> nurse when it wants to get anything out of her*)

HIGGINS

(*Brusquely, recognizing her with unconcealed disap-
pointment, and at once, babylike, making an intolerable
grievance of it*) Why, this is the girl I jotted down last
night. She's no use: I've got all the records I want of the
Lisson Grove lingo, and I'm not going to waste another
cylinder on it. (*To the girl*) Be off with you: I don't
want you.

ELIZA

Don't be so saucy. You ain't heard what I come for yet.
(*To* MRS. PEARCE, *who is waiting at the door for further
instructions*) Did you tell him I come in a taxi?

MRS. PEARCE

Nonsense, girl! What do you think a gentleman like Mr.
Higgins cares what you came in?

ELIZA

Oh, we are proud! He ain't above giving lessons, not
him: I heard him say so. Well, I ain't come here to ask
for any compliment; and if my money's not good enough
I can go elsewhere.

HIGGINS
Good enough for what?

ELIZA
Good enough for ye-oo. Now you know, don't you? I'm come to have lessons, I am. And to pay for 'em too: make no mistake.

HIGGINS
(*Stunned*) Well!!! (*Recovering his breath with a gasp*) What do you expect me to say to you?

ELIZA
Well, if you was a gentleman, you might ask me to sit down, I think. Don't I tell you I'm bringing you business?

HIGGINS
Pickering, shall we ask this baggage to sit down, or shall we throw her out of the window?

ELIZA
(*Running away in terror*) Ah-ah-oh-ow-ow-ow-oo!
(*Wounded and whimpering*) I won't be called a baggage when I've offered to pay like any lady!

PICKERING
(*Gently*) What is it you want, my girl?

ELIZA
I want to be a lady in a flower shop stead of selling at the corner of Tottenham Court Road. But they won't take me unless I can talk more genteel. He said he could teach me. Well, here I am ready to pay him—not asking any favor—and he treats me as if I was dirt. I know what lessons cost as well as you do; and I'm ready to pay.

HIGGINS
How much?

ELIZA
(*Coming back to him, triumphant*) Now you're talking! I thought you'd come off it when you saw a chance of getting back a bit of what you chucked at me last night. (*Confidentially*) You'd had a drop in, hadn't you?

HIGGINS
(*Peremptorily*) Sit down.

ELIZA

Oh, if you're going to make a compliment of it—

HIGGINS

(*Thundering at her*) Sit down.

MRS. PEARCE

(*Severely*) Sit down, girl. Do as you're told.

PICKERING

(*Gently*) What is your name?

ELIZA

Eliza Doolittle.

PICKERING

Won't you sit down, Miss Doolittle?

ELIZA

(*Coyly*) Oh, I don't mind if I do. (*She sits down on sofa*)

HIGGINS

How much do you propose to pay me for the lessons?

ELIZA

Oh, I know what's right. A lady friend of mine gets French lessons for heighteen pence an hour from a real French gentleman. Well, you wouldn't have the face to ask me the same for teaching me my own language as you would for French; so I won't give more than a shilling. Take it or leave it.

HIGGINS

You know, Pickering, if you consider a shilling, not as a simple shilling, but as a percentage of this girl's income, it works out as fully equivalent to sixty or seventy pounds from a millionaire. By George, it's the biggest offer I ever had.

ELIZA

(*Rising, terrified*) Sixty pounds! What are you talkin' about? I never offered you sixty pounds! Where would I get . . .

HIGGINS

Oh, hold your tongue.

ELIZA
(*Weeping*) But I ain't got sixty pounds. Oh . . .

MRS. PEARCE
Don't cry, you silly girl. Sit down. Nobody is going to touch your money.

HIGGINS
Somebody is going to touch you with a broomstick, if you don't stop snivelling. Now, sit down.

ELIZA
Aoooow! One would think you was my father!

HIGGINS
If I decide to teach you, I'll be worse than two fathers to you. Here— (*He offers her his silk handkerchief*)

ELIZA
What's this for?

HIGGINS
To wipe your eyes. To wipe any part of your face that feels moist. Remember, that's your handkerchief; and that's your sleeve. Don't mistake the one for the other if you wish to become a lady in a shop.

PICKERING
Higgins, I'm interested. What about your boast that you could pass her off as a duchess at the Embassy Ball? I'll say you're the greatest teacher alive if you can make that good. I'll bet you all the expenses of the experiment you can't do it. And I'll even pay for the lessons.

ELIZA
Oh, you're real good. Thank you, Captain.

HIGGINS
(*Tempted, looking at her*) It's almost irresistible. She's so deliciously low—so horribly dirty!

ELIZA
Aoooow! I ain't dirty: I washed my face and hands afore I come, I did.

HIGGINS
I'll take it! I'll make a duchess of this draggle-tailed gutter-snipe!

ELIZA
Aoooooooow!

HIGGINS
(*Carried away*) I'll start today! Now! This moment!
Take her away and clean her, Mrs. Pearce. Sandpaper
if it won't come off any other way. Is there a good fire
in the kitchen?

MRS. PEARCE
Yes, but—

HIGGINS
(*Storming on*) Take all her clothes off and burn them.
Ring up and order some new ones. Wrap her up in
brown paper till they come.

ELIZA
You're no gentleman, you're not, to talk of such things.
I'm a good girl, I am; and I know what the likes of you
are, I do.

HIGGINS
We want none of your slum prudery here, young
woman. You've got to learn to behave like a duchess.
Take her away, Mrs. Pearce. If she gives you any
trouble, wallop her.

ELIZA
I'll call the police, I will!

MRS. PEARCE
But I've got no place to put her.

HIGGINS
Put her in the dustbin.

ELIZA
Aooooow!

PICKERING
Oh come, Higgins! Be reasonable.

MRS. PEARCE
You must be reasonable, Mr. Higgins, really you must.
You can't walk over everybody like this.
    (HIGGINS *thus scolded subsides. The hurricane is
    succeeded by a zephyr of amiable surprise*)

HIGGINS

(*With professional exquisiteness of modulation*) I walk over everybody? My dear Mrs. Pearce, my dear Pickering. I never had the slightest intention of walking over anybody. All I propose is that we should be kind to this poor girl. If I did not express myself clearly it was because I did not wish to hurt her delicacy, or yours.

MRS. PEARCE

But, sir, you can't take a girl up like that as if you were picking up a pebble on the beach.

HIGGINS

Why not?

MRS. PEARCE

Why not? But you don't know anything about her! What about her parents? She may be married.

ELIZA

Garn!

HIGGINS

There! As the girl very properly says: Garn!

ELIZA

Who'd marry me?

HIGGINS

(*Suddenly resorting to the most thrillingly beautiful low tones in his best elocutionary style*) By George, Eliza, the streets will be strewn with the bodies of men shooting themselves for your sake before I've done with you.

ELIZA

Here! I'm goin' away! He's off his chump, he is. I don't want no balmies teachin' me.

HIGGINS

(*Wounded in his tenderest point by her insensibility to his elocution*) Oh, indeed! I'm mad, am I? Very well, Mrs. Pearce, you needn't order the new clothes for her. Throw her out! (*He deftly retrieves his handkerchief*)

MRS. PEARCE

Stop, Mr. Higgins! I won't allow it. Go home to your parents, girl.

ELIZA

I ain't got no parents.

HIGGINS

There you are. "She ain't got no parents." What's all
the fuss about? The girl doesn't belong to anybody, and
she's no use to anybody but me. Take her upstairs
and—

MRS. PEARCE

But what's to become of her? Is she to be paid anything? Oh, do be sensible, sir.

HIGGINS

(*Impatiently*) What on earth will she want with money?
She'll have her food and her clothes. She'll only drink
if you give her money.

ELIZA

(*Turning on him*) Oh, you are a brute. It's a lie; nobody ever saw the sign of liquor on me. (*To* PICKERING)
Oh, sir, you're a gentleman; don't let him speak to me
like that!

PICKERING

(*In good-humored remonstrance*) Does it occur to you,
Higgins, that the girl has some feelings?

HIGGINS

(*Looking critically at her*) Oh, no, I don't think so.
Not any feelings that we need bother about. (*Cheerily*)
Have you, Eliza?

MRS. PEARCE

Mr. Higgins. I must know on what terms the girl is to
be here. What is to become of her when you've finished
your teaching? You must look ahead a little, sir.

HIGGINS

What's to become of her if I leave her in the gutter?
Answer me that, Mrs. Pearce.

MRS. PEARCE

That's her own business, not yours, Mr. Higgins.

HIGGINS

Well, when I've done with her, we can throw her back
into the gutter, and then it will be her own business

again; so that's all right. (*He is moved to a chuckle by his own little pleasantry*)

ELIZA

Oh, you've no feelin' heart in you: you don't care for nothing but yourself. Here! I've had enough of this. I'm going. (*She makes for the door*)

HIGGINS

(*Taking her by the arm*) Eliza! (*Snatching a chocolate cream from the table, his eyes suddenly twinkling with mischief*) Have some chocolates.

ELIZA

(*Halting, tempted*) How do I know what might be in them? I've heard of girls being drugged by the like of you.

(HIGGINS *breaks the chocolate in two, puts one half into his mouth and bolts it*)

HIGGINS

Pledge of good faith, Eliza. I eat one half and you eat the other. (ELIZA *opens her mouth to retort.* HIGGINS *pops the chocolate into it*) You shall have boxes of them, barrels of them, every day. You shall live on them, eh?

ELIZA

(*Her mouth full*) I wouldn't have ate it, only I'm too ladylike to take it out of me mouth.

HIGGINS

(*Taking her by the hand and leading her up the stairs*) Think of it, Eliza. Think of chocolates, and taxis, and gold, and diamonds. (*They reach the balcony*)

ELIZA

No! I don't want no gold and no diamonds. I'm a good girl, I am.

PICKERING

Excuse me, Higgins, but I really must interfere! Mrs. Pearce is quite right. If this girl is to put herself in your hands for six months for an experiment in teaching, she must understand thoroughly what she's doing!

HIGGINS

(*Impressed with* PICKERING'S *logic, considers for a*

moment) Eliza, you are to stay here for the next six months learning how to speak beautifully, like a lady in a florist's shop. If you're good and do whatever you're told, you shall sleep in a proper bedroom and have lots to eat, and money to buy chocolates and take rides in taxis. If you're naughty and idle you will sleep in the back kitchen among the black beetles, and be walloped by Mrs. Pearce with a broomstick. At the end of six months you shall go to Buckingham Palace in a carriage, beautifully dressed. If the King finds out you're not a lady, you will be taken by the police to the Tower of London where your head will be cut off as a warning to other presumptuous flower girls. If you are not found out, you shall have a present of seven-and-six to start life with as a lady in a shop. If you refuse this offer you will be the most ungrateful, wicked girl; and the angels will weep for you. (*To* PICKERING) Now are you satisfied, Pickering? (*To* MRS. PEARCE) Could I put it more plainly or fairly, Mrs. Pearce?

MRS. PEARCE
(*Resigned, starts up the stairs*) Come with me, Eliza.

HIGGINS
That's right, Mrs. Pearce. Bundle her off to the bathroom.

ELIZA
(*Reluctantly and suspiciously*) You're a great bully, you are. I won't stay here if I don't like. And I won't let nobody wallop me.

MRS. PEARCE
Don't answer back, girl. (*She leads* ELIZA *through the door*)

ELIZA
(*As she goes*) If I'd known what I was lettin' myself in for, I wouldn't have come up here. I've always been a good girl and I won't be put upon . . . (*She follows* MRS. PEARCE *out the door*)

HIGGINS
(*Coming down the stairs*) In six months—in three if she has a good ear and a quick tongue—I'll take her anywhere and pass her off as anything. I'll make a queen of that barbarous wretch.

PICKERING

Higgins, forgive the bluntness, but if I'm to be in this business, I shall feel responsible for the girl. I hope it's clearly understood that no advantage is to be taken of her position.

HIGGINS

What? That thing? Sacred, I assure you.

PICKERING

(*Gravely*) Now come, Higgins, you know what I mean! This is no trifling matter! Are you a man of good character where women are concerned?

HIGGINS

Have you ever met a man of good character where women were concerned?

PICKERING

Yes. Very frequently.

HIGGINS

(*Dogmatically*) Well, I haven't. I find that the moment I let a woman make friends with me she becomes jealous, exacting, suspicious and a damned nuisance. I find that the moment I let myself become friends with a woman, I become selfish and tyrannical. So here I am, a confirmed old bachelor, and likely to remain so. After all, Pickering . . .

I'm an ordinary man;
Who desires nothing more
Than just the ordinary chance
To live exactly as he likes
And do precisely what he wants.
An average man am I
Of no eccentric whim;
Who likes to live his life
Free of strife,
Doing whatever he thinks is best for him.
Just an ordinary man.

But let a woman in your life
And your serenity is through!
She'll redecorate your home
From the cellar to the dome;

Then get on to the enthralling
Fun of overhauling
You.

Oh, let a woman in your life
And you are up against the wall!
Make a plan and you will find
She has something else in mind;
And so rather than do either
You do something else that neither
Likes at all.

You want to talk of Keats or Milton;
She only wants to talk of love.
You go to see a play or ballet,
And spend it searching for her glove.

Oh, let a woman in your life
And you invite eternal strife!
Let them buy their wedding bands
For those anxious little hands;
I'd be equally as willing
For a dentist to be drilling
Than to ever let a woman in my life!

(*With sudden amiability*)
I'm a very gentle man;
Even-tempered and good-natured,
Whom you never hear complain;
Who has the milk of human kindness
By the quart in ev'ry vein.
A patient man am I
Down to my fingertips;
The sort who never could,
Ever would,
Let an insulting remark escape his lips.

(*Violently*)
But let a woman in your life
And patience hasn't got a chance.
She will beg you for advice;
Your reply will be concise.
And she'll listen very nicely
Then go out and do precisely
What she wants!

You were a man of grace and polish
Who never spoke above a hush.
Now all at once you're using language
That would make a sailor blush.

Oh, let a woman in your life
And you are plunging in a knife!
Let the others of my sex
Tie the knot—around their necks;
I'd prefer a new edition
Of the Spanish Inquisition
Than to ever let a woman in my life!

    (*The storm over, he "cheeps" sweetly to the bird*)
I'm a quiet living man
Who prefers to spend his evenings
In the silence of his room;
Who likes an atmosphere as restful
As an undiscovered tomb.
A pensive man am I
Of philosophic joys;
Who likes to meditate,
Contemplate,
Free from humanity's mad, inhuman noise.
Just a quiet living man.

    (*With abrupt rage*)
But let a woman in your life
And your sabbatical is through!
In a line that never ends
Come an army of her friends;
Come to jabber and to chatter
And to tell her what the matter
Is with you.

She'll have a booming, boist'rous fam'ly
Who will descend on you en masse.
She'll have a large Wagnerian mother
With a voice that shatters glass!

Oh, let a woman in your life . . .
    (*He turns on one of the machines at the accelerated
speed so that the voice coming over the speaker
becomes a piercing female babble. He runs to the
next machine*)

Let a woman in your life . . .
>   (*He turns it on the same way and dashes to the next*)

Let a woman in your life . . .
>   (*He turns on the third; the third being the master control, he slowly turns the volume up until the chattering is unbearable.* PICKERING *covers his ears, his face knotted in pain. Having illustrated his point,* HIGGINS *suddenly turns all the machines off and makes himself comfortable in a chair*)

I shall never let a woman in my life!
>   (*The lights black out for the end of the scene*)

Scene 4

>   The tenement section, Tottenham Court Road, the same as Act One, Scene 2.

TIME: *Noon, three days later.*

AT RISE: MRS. HOPKINS, *a disheveled Cockney lady, has been imparting some juicy gossip to a group of delighted neighbors. She is holding a bird cage and a Chinese fan.*

MRS. HOPKINS
How'd ya like that? Knocked me fer a row of pins, it did.
>   (GEORGE, *the bartender, forcibly evicts* HARRY *and* JAMIE *and then calls into the pub*)

GEORGE
Come on, Doolittle. Out you go. Hop it now. I ain't runnin' no charity bazaar.

DOOLITTLE
(*Coming from the pub*) Thanks for your hospitality, George. Send . . .

GEORGE
Yes, I know. Send the bill to Buckingham Palace. (*He goes back into the pub*)

MRS. HOPKINS

You can buy your own drinks now, Alfie Doolittle. Fallen into a tub of butter, you have.

DOOLITTLE

What tub of butter?

MRS. HOPKINS

Your daughter, Eliza. Oh, you're a lucky man, Alfie Doolittle.

DOOLITTLE

What are you talkin' about? What about Eliza?

MRS. HOPKINS

(*To the crowd*) He don't know. Her own father, and he don't know. (*She and her friends have a good laugh at this*) Moved in with a swell, Eliza has. Left here in a taxi all by herself, smart as paint, and ain't been home for three days. And then I gets a message from her this morning: she wants her things sent over to 27-A Wimpole Street, care of Professor Higgins. And what things does she want? Her bird cage, and her Chinese fan. (*She hands them to* DOOLITTLE) But, she says, never mind about sendin' any clothes! (*She, her friends and* HARRY *and* JAMIE *laugh uproariously.* DOO-LITTLE'S *face shines with paternal pride and the pros- pect of prosperous days*)

DOOLITTLE

I knowed she had a career in front of her! Harry, boy, we're in for a booze-up. The sun is shinin' on Alfred P. Doolittle!

A man was made to help support his children,
Which is the right and proper thing to do.
A man was made to help support his children—but
With a little bit of luck,
With a little bit of luck,
They'll go out and start supporting you!

ALL

With a little bit ... with a little bit ...
With a little bit of luck,
They'll work for you.

He doesn't have a tuppence in his pocket.

The poorest bloke you'll ever hope to meet.
He doesn't have a tuppence in his pocket—but
With a little bit of luck,
With a little bit of luck,
He'll be movin' up to easy street.

With a little bit . . . with a little bit . . .
With a little bit of luck,
He's movin' up.
With a little bit . . . with a little bit . . .
With a little bit of bloomin' luck!
>   (*To the cheers of the crowd,* DOOLITTLE *trips gaily
>   off, a man on the way to El Dorado*)

Scene 5

HIGGINS' *study.*

TIME: *Later that afternoon.*

AT RISE: PICKERING *is seated in the wing chair, reading
            his paper.* MRS. PEARCE *is standing near the
            desk holding some letters in her hand.* HIGGINS
            *is on the balcony engrossed in a bit of re-
            search*)

MRS. PEARCE
   (*Sternly*) Mr. Higgins, you simply cannot go on working the girl this way. Making her say her alphabet over
   and over, from sunup to sundown, even during meals—
   when will it stop?

HIGGINS
   (*Detached but still logical*) When she does it properly,
   of course. Is that all, Mrs. Pearce?

MRS. PEARCE
   No, sir. The mail.

HIGGINS
   Pay the bills and say no to the invitations.

MRS. PEARCE
   There's another letter from that American million-

aire, Ezra D. Wallingford. He still wants you to lecture for his Moral Reform League.

HIGGINS
Throw it away.

MRS. PEARCE
(*Not to be put off*) It's the third letter he's written you, sir. You should at least answer it.

HIGGINS
(*Anything for peace*) Oh, all right. Leave it on the desk. I'll get to it.
    (MRS. PEARCE *places the letter on the desk. While she is doing so, the* BUTLER *enters and addresses* HIGGINS *on the landing*)

BUTLER
If you please, sir, there's a dustman downstairs, Alfred Doolittle, who wants to see you. He says you have his daughter here.

PICKERING
(*Coming to life*) Phew! I say!

HIGGINS
(*Promptly*) Send the blackguard up.
    (*The* BUTLER *goes*)

PICKERING
He may not be a blackguard, Higgins.

HIGGINS
Nonsense. Of course he's a blackguard.

PICKERING
Whether he is or not, I'm afraid we shall have some trouble with him.

HIGGINS
(*Confidently*) Oh no, I think not. If there's any trouble he shall have it with me, not I with him.
    (*The* BUTLER *returns*)

BUTLER
Doolittle, sir.
    (DOOLITTLE *enters and gravely addresses* PICKERING)

DOOLITTLE
  Professor 'iggins?
      (*The* BUTLER *goes*)

HIGGINS
  (*From the balcony*) Here!
      (DOOLITTLE *looks up, momentarily shaken*)

DOOLITTLE
  Morning, Governor. I come about a very serious matter,
  Governor.

HIGGINS
  (*To* PICKERING) Born in Houndslow, mother Welsh!
  (*To* DOOLITTLE) What do you want, Doolittle?

DOOLITTLE
  (*Menacingly*) I want my daughter. That's what I want.
  See?

HIGGINS
  Of course you do. You're her father, aren't you? I'm
  glad to see you have some spark of family feeling
  left. She's upstairs, here. Take her away at once.

DOOLITTLE
  (*Fearfully taken aback*) What??!!

HIGGINS
  Take her away. Do you suppose I'm going to keep
  your daughter for you?

DOOLITTLE
  (*Remonstrating*) Now, now, look here, Governor. Is
  this reasonable? Is it fairity to take advantage of a man
  like this? The girl belongs to me. You got her. Where
  do I come in?

HIGGINS
  (*Charging down the stairs*) How dare you come here
  and attempt to blackmail me? You sent her here on
  purpose.

DOOLITTLE
  (*Protesting*) Now don't take a man up like that, Governor.

HIGGINS

The police shall take you up. This is a plant—a plot to extort money by threats. I shall telephone the police. (*He goes resolutely to the telephone on the desk*)

DOOLITTLE

Have I asked you for a brass farthing? I leave it to this gentleman here. (*To* PICKERING) Have I said a word about money?

HIGGINS

What else did you come for?

DOOLITTLE

(*Sweetly*) Well, what would a man come for? Be human, Governor. (*He wheezes genially in* HIGGINS' *face and rocks him back several paces*)

HIGGINS

(*Recovering*) Alfred, you sent her here on purpose?

DOOLITTLE

So help me, Governor, I never did.

HIGGINS

Then how did you know she was here?

DOOLITTLE

I'll tell ya, Governor, if you'll only let me get a word in. I'm willing to tell ya. I'm wanting to tell ya. I'm waiting to tell ya.

HIGGINS

Pickering, this chap has a certain natural gift of rhetoric. Observe the rhythm of his native woodnotes wild: "I'm willing to tell you; I'm wanting to tell you; I'm waiting to tell you." That's the Welsh strain in him. (*To* DOOLITTLE) How did you know Eliza was here if you didn't send her?

DOOLITTLE

She sent back for her luggage, and I got to hear about it. She said she didn't want no clothes. What was I to think from that, Governor. I ask you as a parient, what was I to think?

HIGGINS

So you came to rescue her from worse than death, eh?

DOOLITTLE

(*Relieved at being so well understood*) Just so, Governor. That's right.

HIGGINS

Mrs. Pearce, Eliza's father has come to take her away. Give her to him.

DOOLITTLE

(*Desperately*) Now wait a minute, Governor, wait a minute. You and me is men of the world, ain't we?

HIGGINS

Oh! Men of the world, are we? You'd better go, Mrs. Pearce.

MRS. PEARCE

I think so indeed, sir! (*She goes with dignity*)

DOOLITTLE

Governor, I've taken a sort of fancy to you. (*Again he wheezes in* HIGGINS' *face, causing the latter almost to lose balance*) And if you want the girl I'm not so set on havin' her back home again, but what I might be open to is an arrangement. All I ask is my rights as a father; and you're the last man alive to expect me to let her go for nothing; for I can see you're one of the straight sort, Governor. Well, what's a five-pound note to you? And what's Eliza to me?

PICKERING

I think you ought to know, Doolittle, that Mr. Higgins' intentions are entirely honorable.

DOOLITTLE

(*To* PICKERING) Of course they are, Governor. If I thought they wasn't, I'd ask fifty.

HIGGINS

(*Revolted*) Do you mean to say that you would sell your daughter for fifty pounds?

PICKERING

Have you no morals, man?

DOOLITTLE

(*Frankly*) No! I can't afford 'em, Governor. Neither could you if you was as poor as me. Not that I mean any harm, mind ya . . . but . . . if Eliza is going to get a bit out of this, why not me, too? Eh? Look at it my way. What am I? I ask ya, what am I? I'm one of the undeserving poor, that's what I am. Think what that means to a man. It means he's up agenst middle-class morality for all the time. If there's anything going and I put in for a bit of it, it's always the same story: you're undeserving, so you can't have it. But my needs is as great as the most deserving widow's that ever got money out of six different charities in one week for the death of the same husband. I don't need less than a deserving man, I need more. I don't eat less hearty than he does, and I drink a lot more. I'm playing straight with you. I ain't pretending to be deserving. I'm undeserving, and I mean to go on being undeserving. I like it, and that's the truth. But will you take advantage of a man's nature to do him out of the price of his own daughter what he's brought up, fed and clothed by the sweat of his brow, till she's growed big enough to be interesting to you two gentlemen? Is five pounds unreasonable? I put it to you, and I leave it to you.

HIGGINS
You know, Pickering, if we were to take this man in hand for three months, he could choose between a seat in the Cabinet and a popular pulpit in Wales. I suppose we ought to give him a fiver?

PICKERING
He'll make bad use of it, I'm afraid.

DOOLITTLE
Not me, so help me, Governor, I won't. Just one good spree for myself and the missus, givin' pleasure to ourselves and employment to others, and satisfaction to you to know it ain't been throwed away. You couldn't spend it better.

HIGGINS
This is irresistible. Let's give him ten. (*He goes to his desk for his wallet*)

DOOLITTLE
No! The missus wouldn't have the heart to spend ten, Governor; ten pounds is a lot of money: it makes a

man feel prudent-like; and then goodbye to happiness.
No, you give me what I ask for, Governor: not a
penny less, not a penny more.

PICKERING

I rather draw the line at encouraging this sort of im-
morality. Doolittle, why don't you marry that missus of
yours? After all, marriage is not so frightening. You
married Eliza's mother?

DOOLITTLE

Who told you that, Governor?

PICKERING

(*Stunned*) Well, nobody told me. But I concluded
naturally . . .
        (DOOLITTLE *emphatically shakes his head to the
        contrary*)

HIGGINS

(*Returning with a five-pound note*) Pickering, if we
listen to this man another minute we shall have no con-
victions left. Five pounds, I think you said?

DOOLITTLE

(*Taking it*) Thank you, Governor.
        (*He hurries for the door, anxious to get away with
        his booty. In the rush, he collides with a rather
        nicely dressed, clean, but angry young woman
        with a copy book in her hand. It is, of course,
        ELIZA whom he does not recognize. MRS. PEARCE
        is with her*)

ELIZA

(*In a rage*) I won't! I won't! I won't!

DOOLITTLE

(*At the collision*) Beg pardon, Miss!

ELIZA

(*Ignoring him and confronting* HIGGINS) I won't say
those ruddy vowels one more time!

DOOLITTLE

Blimey, it's Eliza! I never thought she'd clean up so
good-lookin'. She does me credit, don't she, Governor?

ELIZA

(*Her anger heightened by his presence*) Here! What are you doin' here?

DOOLITTLE

(*Sternly*) You hold your tongue and don't you give these gentlemen none of your lip. If you have any trouble with her, Governor, give her a few licks of the strap. That's the way to improve her mind. (*He bows low*) Good mornin', gentlemen. (*Cheerfully whacking* ELIZA *on the backside*) Cheerio, Eliza. (*He goes out the door in such high good spirits he cannot resist laughing out loud*)

HIGGINS

By George, there's a man for you! A philosophical genius of the first water. Mrs. Pearce, write to Mr. Ezra Wallingford and tell him if he wants a lecturer to get in touch with Mr. Alfred P. Doolittle, a common dustman—but one of the most original moralists in England.

MRS. PEARCE

Yes, sir. (*She goes*)

ELIZA

Here, what did he come for?

HIGGINS

Say your vowels.

ELIZA

(*Ready to explode at the mention of them*) I know my vowels. I knew them before I came.

HIGGINS

If you know them, say them.

ELIZA

Ahyee, E, Iyee, Ow, You!

HIGGINS

(*Thundering*) Stop! Say: A, E, I, O, U!

ELIZA

That's what I said: Ahyee, E, Iyee, Ow, You. I've been syin' them for three days, and I won't sy them no more!

PICKERING
(*Gently*) I know it's difficult, Miss Doolittle. But try to understand . . .

HIGGINS
No use explaining, Pickering. As a military man you ought to know that. Drilling is what she needs. Much better leave her or she'll be turning to you for sympathy.

PICKERING
All right, if you insist, but have a little patience with her, Higgins. (*He goes out the door*)

HIGGINS
Of course. (*To* ELIZA) Say "A."

ELIZA
You ain't got no heart, you ain't.

HIGGINS
"A."

ELIZA
Ahyee!

HIGGINS
(*Walks up the stairs saying "A" with each step,* ELIZA *defiantly echoing "Ahyee." When he reaches the landing he addresses her with firm resolve*) Eliza, I promise you you will pronounce your vowels correctly before this day is out, or there'll be no lunch, no dinner, and no chocolates! (*He exits through the door on the landing, punctuating his threat with a slam of the door*)
   (ELIZA, *in a blind rage, slams her study book down on the floor and stamps on it*)

ELIZA
Just you wait, 'enry 'iggins, just you wait!
You'll be sorry but your tears'll be too late!
You'll be broke and I'll have money;
Will I help you? Don't be funny!
Just you wait, 'enry 'iggins, just you wait!

Just you wait, 'enry 'iggins, till you're sick,
And you scream to fetch a doctor double-quick.
I'll be off a second later

And go straight to the the-ater!
Oh ho ho, 'enry 'iggins, just you wait!

Ooooooooh 'enry 'iggins!
Just you wait until we're swimmin' in the sea!
Ooooooooh 'enry 'iggins!
And you get a cramp a little ways from me!

When you yell you're going to drown
I'll get dressed and go to town!
Oh ho ho, 'enry 'iggins!
Oh ho ho, 'enry 'iggins!
Just you wait!

One day I'll be famous! I'll be proper and prim;
Go to St. James so often I will call it St. Jim!
One evening the King will say: "Oh, Liza, old thing,
I want all of England your praises to sing.
Next week on the twentieth of May
I proclaim Liza Doolittle Day!
All the people will celebrate the glory of you,
And whatever you wish and want I gladly will do."

"Thanks a lot, King," says I, in a manner well-bred;
"But all I want is 'enry 'iggins 'ead!"
"Done," says the King, with a stroke.
"Guard, run and bring in the bloke!"

Then they'll march you, 'enry 'iggins, to the wall;
And the King will tell me: "Liza, sound the call."
As they raise their rifles higher,
I'll shout: "Ready! Aim! Fire!"
Oh ho ho! 'enry 'iggins!
Down you'll go! *'enry 'iggins!*
Just you wait!!!

                    Blackout
(*The lights come up in the study.* ELIZA *is on the
stool in front of the desk.* HIGGINS *is in the alcove
repairing a metronome.* PICKERING *as usual is in
the wing chair reading the London* Times)

ELIZA
    The rine in spine sties minely in the pline.

HIGGINS
    (*Correcting her*) The rain in Spain stays mainly in the
    plain.

ELIZA
Didn't I sy that?

HIGGINS
No, Eliza, you didn't "sy" that. You didn't even "say"
that. (*He picks up a small burner and brings it down
to the desk*) Every night before you get into bed, where
you used to say your prayers, I want you to repeat:
"The rain in Spain stays mainly in the plain," fifty
times. You will get much further with the Lord if you
learn not to offend His ears. Now for your "H's." Pickering, this is going to be ghastly!

PICKERING
Control yourself, Higgins. Give the girl a chance.

HIGGINS
(*Patiently*) Of course. No one expects her to get it
right the first time. Watch closely, Eliza. (*He places
the burner on the desk and lights the flame*) You see
this flame? Every time you say your aitch properly, the
flame will waver. Every time you drop your aitch, the
flame will remain stationary. That's how you will know
you've done it correctly; in time your ear will hear the
difference. Now, listen carefully; in Hertford, Hereford
and Hampshire, hurricanes hardly ever happen.
    (ELIZA *sits down behind the desk*)
Now repeat after me, In Hertford, Hereford and Hampshire, hurricanes hardly ever happen.

ELIZA
(*Conscientiously*) In 'ertford, 'ereford and 'ampshire,
'urricanes 'ardly hever 'appen!

HIGGINS
(*Infuriated*) No, no, no, no! Have you no ear at all?

ELIZA
(*Willingly*) Should I do it over?

HIGGINS
No. Please, no! We must start from the very beginning.
(*He kneels before the flame*) Do this: ha, ha, ha, ha.
(*He rises*)

ELIZA
Ha—ha—ha—ha. (*She looks up at him happily*)

HIGGINS

Well, go on. Go on.

(ELIZA *continues.* HIGGINS *strolls casually over to*
PICKERING, *leaving* ELIZA *to aspirate at the flame*)

Does the same thing hold true in India, Pickering; the
peculiar habit of not only dropping a letter like the
letter aitch, but using it where it shouldn't be? Like
"hever" instead of "ever"? You'll notice some of the
Slavic peoples when they learn to speak English have
a tendency to that with their G's. They say "linger"
(soft g) instead of "linger" (hard g); and then they
turn around and say "singer" (hard g) instead of
"singer" (soft g).

(PICKERING *had never thought about it and naturally is perplexed*)

I wonder why that's so. I must look it up.

(HIGGINS *starts for the landing.* ELIZA, *by this
time, is sinking fast from lack of oxygen.* PICKER-
ING *notices her dying gasps and pulls* HIGGINS'
arm to call his attention to it)

(*Thinking which book to consult*)

Go on! Go on!

(*He continues up the stairs.* ELIZA *musters together one final "HA" and blows out the flame.
The room is plunged into darkness*)

(*In the darkness, six* SERVANTS *emerge, and stand
in a spotlight at the far end of the study*)

SERVANTS

Poor Professor Higgins!
Poor Professor Higgins!
Night and day
He slaves away!
Oh, poor Professor Higgins!
All day long
On his feet;
Up and down until he's numb;
Doesn't rest;
Doesn't eat;
Doesn't touch a crumb!

(*The spotlight goes off. The servants disappear
and the lights come up in the study.* PICKERING *is
seated in his favorite chair with a large and ful-
some tea table before him.* ELIZA *is on the sofa.*

HIGGINS *is standing by the xylophone, a cup in
one hand, a xylophone mallet in the other. He taps
out eight notes. "How kind of you to let me
come.")*

HIGGINS

Kind of you, *kind* of you, *kind* of you. Now listen,
Eliza. (*He plays them again*) How kind of you to let
me come.

ELIZA

How kind of *you* to let me come.

HIGGINS

(*Puts down the mallet in despair and walks over to the
tea table*) No! *Kind* of you. It's just like *"cup* of tea."
Kind of you—*cup* of tea. *Kind* of you—Say "cup of
tea."

ELIZA

(*Hungrily*) Cappatea.

HIGGINS

No! No! A cup of tea . . . (*Takes a mouthful of cake
from the tray*) It's awfully good cake. I wonder where
Mrs. Pearce gets it?

PICKERING

Mmmmm! First rate! The strawberry tarts are delicious.
And did you try the pline cake? (HIGGINS *looks at him
in horror and then turns to* ELIZA)

HIGGINS

Now, try it again, Eliza. A cup of tea. A cup of tea.

ELIZA

(*Longingly*) A cappatea.

HIGGINS

Can't you hear the difference? Put your tongue forward
until it squeezes against the top of your lower teeth.
Now say "cup."

ELIZA

(*Her attention only on the cake in* HIGGINS' *hand*)
C-cup.

HIGGINS

Now say "of."

ELIZA

   Of.

HIGGINS

   Now say, cup, cup, cup, cup—of, of, of, of.

ELIZA

   Cup, cup, cup, cup—of, of, of, of! Cup, cup, cup, cup—of, of, of, of . . .

PICKERING

   (*As she's practicing*) By Jove, that was a glorious tea, Higgins. Do finish the strawberry tart. I couldn't eat another thing.

HIGGINS

   No, thanks, old chap, really.

PICKERING

   It's a shame to waste it.

HIGGINS

   Oh, it won't go to waste. (*He takes the last tart*) I know someone who's immensely fond of strawberry tarts.

      (ELIZA'S *eyes light up hopefully. But alas,* HIGGINS *walks right past her and goes to the bird cage*)

HIGGINS

   (*Pushing the cake thru the bars*) Cheep, cheep, cheep!

ELIZA

   (*Shrieking*) Aaaaaaaaaaaooooooooooowwww!!
                 Blackout
      (*The lights black out and the* SERVANTS *again appear in the spotlight*)

SERVANTS

   Poor Professor Higgins!
   Poor Professor Higgins!
   On he plods
   Against all odds;
   Oh, poor Professor Higgins!
   Nine P.M.
   Ten P.M.
   On through midnight ev'ry night.
   One A.M.

TWO A.M.
Three . . . !

(The spotlight goes off. The SERVANTS *disappear and the lights come up again in the study.* ELIZA *is seated in the wing chair.* HIGGINS *has drawn up the stool and is facing her, a small box of marbles in his hand. He is placing them in her mouth)*

HIGGINS

Four . . . five . . . six marbles. There we are. *(He holds up a slip of paper)* Now, I want you to read this and enunciate each word just as if the marbles were not in your mouth. "With blackest moss, the flower pots were thickly crusted, one and all." Each word clear as a bell. *(He gives her the paper)*

ELIZA

(Unintelligibly) With blackest moss the flower pots . . . I can't! I can't!

PICKERING

(From the sofa) I say, Higgins, are those pebbles really necessary?

HIGGINS

If they were necessary for Demosthenes, they are necessary for Eliza Doolittle. Go on, Eliza.

ELIZA

(Trying again with no better results) With blackest moss, the flower pots were thickly crusted, one and all. . . .

HIGGINS

I cannot understand a word. Not a word.

ELIZA

(Her anger coming thru the marbles and "flowerpots") With blackest moss, the flower pots were thickly crusted, one and all; the rusted nails fell from the knots that held the pear to the gable-wall . . .

PICKERING

(Soon after she has begun) I say, Higgins, perhaps the poem is too difficult for the girl. Why don't you try a simpler one, like: "The Owl and the Pussycat"? Oh, yes, that's a charming one.

HIGGINS

(*Bellowing*) Pickering! I cannot hear the girl!

(ELIZA *gasps and takes the marbles out of her mouth*)

What's the matter? Why did you stop?

ELIZA

I swallowed one.

HIGGINS

(*Reassuringly*) Oh, don't worry. I have plenty more. Open your mouth.

(*The lights go out and into the spotlight again appear the* SERVANTS)

SERVANTS

Quit, Professor Higgins!
Quit, Professor Higgins!
Hear our plea
Or payday we
Will quit, Professor Higgins!
Ay not I,
O not Ow,
Pounding, pounding in our brain.
Ay not I,
O, not Ow,
Don't say "Rine," say "Rain" . . .

(*The spotlight goes off. The* SERVANTS *disappear and the lights come up again on the study.* ELIZA *is draped wearily on the sofa.* PICKERING *is half asleep in the wing chair.* HIGGINS *is seated at his desk, an ice-bag on his head. The gray light outside the windows indicates the early hours of the morning*)

HIGGINS

(*Wearily*) The rain in Spain stays mainly in the plain.

ELIZA

I can't. I'm so tired. I'm so tired.

PICKERING

(*Half asleep*) Oh, for heaven's sake, Higgins. It must be three o'clock in the morning. Do be reasonable.

HIGGINS

(*Rising*) I am always reasonable. Eliza, if I can go on with a blistering headache, you can.

ELIZA

I have a headache, too.

HIGGINS

Here.

> (*He plops the ice-bag on her head. She takes it off her head and buries her face in her hands, exhausted to the point of tears*)

(*With sudden gentleness*) Eliza, I know you're tired. I know your head aches. I know your nerves are as raw as meat in a butcher's window. But think what you're trying to accomplish. (*He sits next to her on sofa*) Think what you're dealing with. The majesty and grandeur of the English language. It's the greatest possession we have. The noblest sentiments that ever flowed in the hearts of men are contained in its extraordinary, imaginative and musical mixtures of sounds. That's what you've set yourself to conquer, Eliza. And conquer it you will. (*He rises, goes to the chair behind his desk and seats himself heavily*) Now, try it again.

ELIZA

(*Slowly*) The rain in Spain stays mainly in the plain.

HIGGINS

(*Sitting up*) What was that?

ELIZA

The rain in Spain stays mainly in the plain.

HIGGINS

(*Rising, unbelievably*) Again.

ELIZA

The rain in Spain stays mainly in the plain.

HIGGINS

(*To* PICKERING)
I think she's got it! think she's got it!

ELIZA

The rain in Spain stays mainly in the plain.

HIGGINS
(*Triumphantly*)
By George, she's got it!
By George, she's got it!
Now once again, where does it rain?

ELIZA
On the plain! On the plain!

HIGGINS
And where's that soggy plain?

ELIZA
In Spain! In Spain!
(PICKERING *jumps to his feet and the three sing out joyously*)

THE THREE
The rain in Spain stays mainly in the plain!
The rain in Spain stays mainly in the plain!
(HIGGINS *walks excitedly to the xylophone*)

HIGGINS
In Hertford, Hereford and Hampshire . . . ?

ELIZA
Hurricanes hardly happen.

HIGGINS
(*Taps out "How kind of you to let me come"*)

ELIZA
How kind of you to let me come!

HIGGINS
(*Putting down the mallet and turning back to her*)
Now once again, where does it rain?

ELIZA
On the plain! On the plain!

HIGGINS
And where's that blasted plain?

ELIZA
In Spain! In Spain!

THE THREE
The rain in Spain stays mainly in the plain!

The rain in Spain stays mainly in the plain!

(*Joy and victory!* HIGGINS *takes a handkerchief from his pocket and waves it in front of* PICKERING *who charges it like the finest bull in Spain.* HIGGINS *turns and grabs* ELIZA *and they do a few awkward tango steps while* PICKERING *jumps around like a flamenco dancer shouting "Viva Higgins, Viva."* HIGGINS *swings* ELIZA *onto the sofa and joins* PICKERING *in a bit of heel-clicking.* ELIZA *jumps down from the sofa. They throw themselves into a wild jig and then all collapse back upon the sofa engulfed in laughter*)

(MRS. PEARCE *enters in her nightrobe, followed by two of the* SERVANTS *who have also been awakened*)

HIGGINS

Pickering, we're making fine progress. I think the time has come to try her out.

MRS. PEARCE

(*Making her presence known*) Are you feeling all right, Mr. Higgins?

HIGGINS

Quite well, thank you, Mrs. Pearce. And you?

MRS. PEARCE

Very well, sir, thank you.

HIGGINS

Splendid. (*To* PICKERING) Let's test her in public and see how she fares.

MRS. PEARCE

Mr. Higgins, I was awakened by a dreadful pounding. Do you know what it might have been?

HIGGINS

Pounding? I heard no pounding. Did you, Pickering?

PICKERING

(*Innocently*) No.

HIGGINS

If this continues, Mrs. Pearce, I should see a doctor. Pickering, I know! Let's take her to the races.

PICKERING
(*Rising*) The races!?

HIGGINS
(*Rising too, excited by the idea*) Yes! My mother's box at Ascot.

PICKERING
(*Cautiously*) You'll consult your mother first, of course.

HIGGINS
Of course. (*Thinking better of it*) No! We'll surprise her. Let's go straight to bed. First thing in the morning we'll go off and buy her a dress. Eliza, go on with your work.

MRS. PEARCE
But Mr. Higgins, it's early in the morning!

HIGGINS
What better time to work than early in the morning? (*To* PICKERING) Where does one buy a lady's gown?

PICKERING
Whiteley's, of course.

HIGGINS
How do you know that?

PICKERING
Common knowledge.

HIGGINS
(*Studying* PICKERING *carefully*) We mustn't get her anything too flowery. I despise those gowns with a sort of weed here and a weed there. Something simple, modest and elegant is what's called for. Perhaps with a sash. (*He places the imaginary sash on* PICKERING'S *hip and steps back to eye it*) Yes. Just right.
  (*He goes out the door.* PICKERING *looks down at his hip to reassure himself the sash is not there and follows after him*)
  (MRS. PEARCE, *whose face has been a study in amazement, goes quickly to* ELIZA)

MRS. PEARCE
You've all been working much too hard. I think the strain is beginning to show. Eliza, I don't care what Mr.

Higgins says, you must put down your books and go to bed.

ELIZA

> (*Lost on an errant cloud only hears her from far below*)

Bed! Bed! I couldn't go to bed!
My head's too light to try to set it down!
Sleep! Sleep! I couldn't sleep tonight!
Not for all the jewels in the crown!

I could have danced all night!
I could have danced all night!
And still have begged for more.
I could have spread my wings
And done a thousand things
I've never done before.

I'll never know
What made it so exciting;
Why all at once
My heart took flight.
I only knew when he
Began to dance with me,
I could have danced, danced, danced all night!

IST SERVANT

> (*To* ELIZA)
It's after three, now.

2ND SERVANT

> (*To* MRS. PEARCE)
Don't you agree, now,
She ought to be in bed?
> (MRS. PEARCE *nods emphatically*)

ELIZA

> (*Telling the servants*)
I could have danced all night!
I could have danced all night!
And still have begged for more.
I could have spread my wings
And done a thousand things
I've never done before.

SERVANTS
(*Simultaneously telling* ELIZA)
You're tired out.
You must be dead.
Your face is drawn.
Your eyes are red.
Now say goodnight, please.
Turn out the light, please.
It's really time.
For you to be in bed.
Do come along.
Do as you're told,
Or Mrs. Pearce
Is apt to scold.
You're up too late, miss.
And sure as fate, miss.
You'll catch a cold.
(MRS. PEARCE *goes to the alcove for a comforter*)

ELIZA
I'll never know
What made it so exciting,
Why all at once
My heart took flight.
I only know when he
Began to dance with me
I could have danced, danced, danced all night!

SERVANTS
(*Simultaneously*)
Put down your book
The work'll keep.
Now settle down
And go to sleep.
(ELIZA *stretches out on the sofa and* MRS. PEARCE
covers her with a comforter)

MRS. PEARCE
I understand, dear.
It's all been grand, dear.
But now it's time to sleep.
(*She turns out the lights and she and the* SERVANTS
go)

ELIZA

> (*Reliving it*)
> I could have danced all night!
> I could have danced all night!
> And still have begged for more.
> I could have spread my wings
> And done a thousand things
> I've never done before.
> I'll never know
> What made it so exciting,
> Why all at once
> My heart took flight.
>> (*She throws off the comforter and jumps to her feet*)
> I only know when he
> Began to dance with me
> I could have danced, danced, danced all night!

Scene 6

> *Near the race meeting, Ascot.*

TIME: *A sunny July afternoon.*

AT RISE: PICKERING, *dressed for Ascot, is strolling toward the club tent with* MRS. HIGGINS. MRS. HIGGINS, *elegantly gowned, is a woman a shade perhaps beyond sixty.* CHARLES, MRS. HIGGINS' *chauffeur, follows dutifully behind.* MRS. HIGGINS, *obviously perplexed by* PICKERING'S *conversation, pauses.*

MRS. HIGGINS

Colonel Pickering, I don't understand. Do you mean that my son is coming to Ascot today?

PICKERING

Yes, he is, Mrs. Higgins. As a matter of fact, he's here!

MRS. HIGGINS

(*Dismayed*) What a disagreeable surprise. Ascot is usually the one place I can come to with my friends and

not run the risk of seeing my son, Henry. Whenever my
friends meet him, I never see them again.

PICKERING
    He had to come, Mrs. Higgins. You see, he's taking the
    girl to the annual Embassy Ball, and he wanted to try
    her out first.

MRS. HIGGINS
    (*Blank bewilderment*) I beg your pardon?

PICKERING
    (*Clearing it up*) You know, the annual Embassy Ball.

MRS. HIGGINS
    Yes, I know the Ball; but what girl?

PICKERING
    Oh, didn't I mention that?

MRS. HIGGINS
    No, you did not.

PICKERING
    Well, it's quite simple, really. One night I went to the
    Opera at Covent Garden to hear one of my favorite
    operas, *Aida;* and as I was coming out incidentally, they
    didn't do *Aida* that night. No, they did *Götterdäm-
    merung* instead. I'd never heard *Götterdämmerung.* By
    George, that's a rackety one! When the tenor chap . . .

MRS. HIGGINS
    (*Impatiently*) What about the girl, Colonel?

PICKERING
    Oh, yes. As I was coming out, I met your son, Henry,
    who, in turn, met Miss Doolittle, who now lives with
    Henry.

MRS. HIGGINS
    Lives with Henry? (*Hopefully*) Is it a love affair?

PICKERING
    Heaven's no! She's a flower girl. He picked her up off the
    kerbstone.

MRS. HIGGINS
    (*Not quite believing her ears*) A flower girl?

PICKERING

Yes. Higgins said to me: "Pickering, you see this girl? In six months I could make a duchess of her." I said: "Nonsense." He came right back with: "Yes, I can." "All right," I said, "I'll make a bet with you you can't." And I did. And he is.

MRS. HIGGINS

But, Colonel, I still don't understand.
(*A distant bell is heard ringing*)

CHARLES

The horses are leaving the paddock, Mrs. Higgins.

PICKERING

Excuse me, Mrs. Higgins. I must fetch her. (*He tips his hat politely and moves and starts off*)

MRS. HIGGINS

But Colonel, am I to understand that Henry is bringing a flower girl to Ascot?

PICKERING

(*Turning, delighted that* MRS. HIGGINS *finally understands*) Yes, Mrs. Higgins! That's it, that's it precisely! Jolly good, Mrs. Higgins! Jolly good!

MRS. HIGGINS

(*Calmly*) Charles, you'd better stay close to the car. I may be leaving abruptly. (*She sweeps off*)

Scene 7

SCENE: *Inside a club tent, Ascot.*

There is an archway in the center and two large pouffes on either side. To view the races one would look out at the mythical "fourth wall".

TIME: *Immediately following.*

AT RISE: *The stage is filled with ladies and gentlemen of Ascot all appropriately attired for the occasion. At this precise moment, they are standing in groups looking out at the race track, the immobility of their faces and bodies registering their abiding disdain from any emotional display.*

LADIES AND GENTLEMEN
Ev'ry duke and earl and peer is here.
Ev'ry one who should be here is here.
What a smashing, positively dashing
Spectacle: the Ascot op'ning day.

At the gate are all the horses
Waiting for the cue to fly away.
What a gripping, absolutely ripping
Moment at the Ascot op'ning day.

Pulses rushing!
Faces flushing!
Heartbeats speed up!
I have never been so keyed up!

Any second now
They'll begin to run.
Hark! a bell is ringing,
They are springing
Forward
Look! It has begun . . . !
(*In stony silence and with a reserve indistinguishable from boredom they observe the progress of the race*)

What a frenzied moment that was!
Didn't they maintain an exhausting pace?
'Twas a thrilling, absolutely chilling
Running of the Ascot op'ning race.
(*To the strains of this Gavotte they move cautiously about, finally disappearing.* MRS. HIGGINS *enters and bows graciously to one or two as they go off. Almost immediately* HIGGINS *enters briskly, dressed in tweeds*)

HIGGINS
(*To himself*) I don't know where the devil they could be. (*He sees his mother and comes to her*) Oh, darling, have you seen Pickering? My, you do look nice! (*Kisses her*)

MRS. HIGGINS

I saw Colonel Pickering, and Henry, dear, I'm most provoked. I've heard you've brought a common flower girl from Covent Garden to my box at Ascot.

HIGGINS

Oh, darling, she'll be all right. I've taught her to speak properly, and she has strict orders as to her behavior. She's to keep to two subjects: the weather and everybody's health—sort of "fine day" and "how do you do", and not just let herself go on things in general. Help her along, darling, and you'll be quite safe.

MRS. HIGGINS

Safe? To talk about our health in the middle of a race?

HIGGINS

(*Impatiently*) Well, she's got to talk about something. (*His eyes wander about in search of them*)

MRS. HIGGINS

Henry, you're not even dressed properly.

HIGGINS

I changed my shirt.

MRS. HIGGINS

Where is the girl now?

HIGGINS

Being pinned. Some of the clothes we bought for her didn't quite fit. I told Pickering we should have taken her with us.

MRS. HIGGINS

You're a pretty pair of babies playing with your live doll.
    (MRS. EYNSFORD-HILL, FREDDY EYNSFORD-HILL
    and LORD *and* LADY BOXINGTON, *an elderly couple,*
    stroll on. MRS. HIGGINS *greets them*)
Ah, Mrs. Eynsford-Hill!

HIGGINS

Oh damn, are all these people with you? (*He walks away*)

MRS. EYNSFORD-HILL

Mrs. Higgins, is this your celebrated son?

MRS. HIGGINS
I'm sorry to say my celebrated son has no manners. He
may be the life and soul of the Royal Society soirées, but
he's rather trying on more commonplace occasions.
  (PICKERING *enters followed by* ELIZA, *who is ex-
  quisitely dressed; she produces an impression of re-
  markable distinction and beauty*)

HIGGINS
(*Seeing them*) Ah!

MRS. HIGGINS
Ah, Colonel Pickering, you're just in time for tea.

PICKERING
Thank you. Mrs. Higgins, may I introduce Miss Eliza
Doolittle?

MRS. HIGGINS
(*Extending her hand graciously*) My dear Miss Doolittle.

ELIZA
(*Speaking with pedantic correctness of pronunciation
and great beauty of tone*) How kind of you to let me
come. (*She says it properly and* HIGGINS *nods his ap-
proval*)

MRS. HIGGINS
Delighted, my dear. (*Introducing*) Mrs. Eynsford-Hill.
Miss Doolittle.

MRS. EYNSFORD-HILL
How do you do?

ELIZA
How do you do? (*She gasps slightly in making sure of
the H in "how" but is quite successful*)

MRS. HIGGINS
(*Introducing*) Lord and Lady Boxington. Miss Doolittle.

LORD AND LADY BOXINGTON
How do you do?

ELIZA
How do you do?

MRS. HIGGINS
(*Introducing*) And Freddy Eynsford-Hill.

ELIZA
How do you do?

FREDDY
(*Instantly infatuated*) How do you do?

HIGGINS
Miss Doolittle?

ELIZA
Good afternoon, Professor Higgins.
> (HIGGINS *motions for her to sit down, she looks at him blankly. He pantomimes sitting down and she does. They all seat themselves on the two pouffes,* ELIZA *finding herself between* MRS. HIGGINS *and* FREDDY. HIGGINS, *of course, stays on his feet.* TWO STEWARDS *serve tea*)

FREDDY
The first race was very exciting, Miss Doolittle. I'm so sorry you missed it.

MRS. HIGGINS
(*Hurriedly*) Will it rain do you think?

ELIZA
The rain in Spain stays mainly in the plain.
> (HIGGINS *irresistibly does a quick fandango step which is so bizarre that the others have nothing to do but pretend it didn't happen*)

But in Hertford, Hereford and Hampshire hurricanes hardly ever happen.

FREDDY
Ha ha, how awfully funny.

ELIZA
What is wrong with that, young man? I bet I got it right.

FREDDY
Smashing!

MRS. EYNSFORD-HILL
I do hope we won't have any unseasonably cold spells. It brings on so much influenza, and our whole family is susceptible to it.

ELIZA

(*Darkly*) My aunt died of influenza, so they said. (MRS. EYNSFORD-HILL *clicks her tongue sympathetically*) But it's my belief they done the old woman in.

(HIGGINS *and* PICKERING *look at each other accusingly as if each blames the other for having taught* ELIZA *this last unrehearsed phrase*)

MRS. HIGGINS

(*Puzzled*) Done her in?

ELIZA

Yes, Lord love you! Why should she die of influenza when she come through diphtheria right enough the year before? Fairly blue with it she was. They all thought she was dead; but my father, he kept ladling gin down her throat.

(HIGGINS, *for want of something to do, balances his tea cup on his head and takes several steps without spilling it. Quite a feat*)

Then she came to so sudden that she bit the bowl off the spoon.

MRS. HIGGINS

(*Startled*) Dear me!

ELIZA

(*Piling up the indictment*) Now, what call would a woman with that strength in her have to die of influenza, and what become of her new straw hat that should have come to me? Somebody pinched it.

(HIGGINS *fans himself with a silver tray off the tea cart*)

And what I say is, them as pinched it, done her in.

LORD BOXINGTON

(*Nervously loud*) Done her in? Done her in, did you say?

HIGGINS

(*Hastily*) Oh, that's the new small talk. To do a person in means to kill them.

MRS. EYNSFORD-HILL

(*To* ELIZA, *horrified*) You surely don't believe your aunt was killed?

ELIZA

Do I not! Them she lived with would have killed her for
a hatpin, let alone a hat.

MRS. EYNSFORD-HILL

But it can't have been right for your father to pour spirits
down her throat like that. It might have killed her.

ELIZA

Not her. Gin was mother's milk to her.

> (PICKERING *stiffens.* HIGGINS *decides to leave, tips
> his hat to all, and starts off. However, his uncon-
> trollable curiosity holds him at the last moment to
> hear what else* ELIZA *has to say*)

Besides, he'd poured so much down his own throat that
he knew the good of it.

LORD BOXINGTON

Do you mean that he drank?

ELIZA

Drank! My word! Something chronic. (*To* FREDDY, *who
is in convulsions of suppressed laughter*) Here! What are
you sniggering at?

FREDDY

The new small talk. You do it so awfully well.

ELIZA

If I was doing it proper, what was you laughing at? (*To*
HIGGINS) Have I said anything I oughtn't?

MRS. HIGGINS

(*Interposing*) Not at all, my dear.

ELIZA

Well, that's a mercy, anyhow. (*Expansively*) What I always say is . . .

> (PICKERING *jumps to his feet. He and* HIGGINS *make
> a number of desperate signals and strange sounds
> to prevent her from going on*)

PICKERING

(*Rushing to* ELIZA) I don't suppose there's enough time
before the next race to place a bet? (*To* ELIZA) Come,
my dear.

> (ELIZA *rises*)

MRS. HIGGINS
I'm afraid not, Colonel Pickering.
>(*They all rise as several of the ladies and gentle-
men enter to take their positions for the next race*)

FREDDY
I have a bet on number seven. I should be so happy if
you would take it. You'll enjoy the race ever so much
more. (*He offers her a race ticket. She accepts*)

ELIZA
That's very kind of you.
>(FREDDY *leads* ELIZA *to a vantage point directly
center*)

FREDDY
His name is Dover.

ELIZA
(*Repeating the name*) Dover.

LADIES *and* GENTLEMEN *and* ALL (*except* HIGGINS)
There they are again
Lining up to run.
Now they're holding steady,
They are ready
For it.
Look! It has begun!
>(*Again the mummified silence. The one exception
is* ELIZA. *Clenching her fists with excitement, she
leans forward. Oblivious to the deportment of those
around her, she begins to cheer her horse on*)

ELIZA
(*At first softly*) Come on, come on, Dover!
>(*The* LADIES *and* GENTLEMEN *slowly turn to stare
at her and look at each other in wonder*)
Come on, come on, Dover!
>(*Her voice crescendoes. The* LADIES *and* GENTLE-
MEN *move perceptively away from this ugly exhibition of natural behavior*)
Come on, Dover!!! Move your bloomin' arse!!!
>(*An agonizing moan rises up from the crowd. The
moment she says it she realizes what she has done
and brings her hand to her mouth as if trying to
push the words back in. Several women gracefully*

faint, and are caught by their escorts. LORD *and* LADY BOXINGTON *are staggered.* PICKERING *flies from the scene running faster than Dover.* HIGGINS, *of course, roars with laughter*)

Scene 8

Outside HIGGINS' *house, Wimpole Street.*

TIME: *Later that day.*

AT RISE: *A* CONSTABLE *is strolling along the street.* FREDDY, *a man with a purpose, walks up to the* CONSTABLE.

FREDDY
  Officer, I know this is Wimpole Street, but could you tell me where 27-A is?

POLICEMAN
  (*Indicating* HIGGINS' *house*) Right there, sir.

FREDDY
  Thank you. (*The* CONSTABLE *strolls on.* FREDDY *starts for the door when a* FLOWER GIRL *passes, looking very much as* ELIZA *used to, carrying a basket of flowers.* FREDDY *stops her*) Are those for sale?

FLOWER GIRL
  Yes, sir. A shilling.
        (FREDDY *takes a shilling from his pocket—his last—and gives it to the* FLOWER GIRL *in exchange for a small nosegay*)

FREDDY
  Here.

FLOWER GIRL
  Thank you kindly, sir.

FREDDY
  (*With radiant good spirits*) Isn't it a heavenly day?
        (*The* FLOWER GIRL *looks up at the sky which is quite overcast. Thinking him undoubtedly mad, she hurries on*)

(FREDDY *knocks on* HIGGINS' *door and while await-ing response, irrepressibly gives vent to his feelings*)

FREDDY

When she mentioned how her aunt bit off the spoon,
She completely done me in.
And my heart went on a journey to the moon,
When she told about her father and the gin.
And I never saw a more enchanting farce,
Than the moment when she shouted "move your
bloomin' " . . .

MRS. PEARCE

(*Opens the door*) Yes, sir?

FREDDY

Is Miss Doolittle at home?

MRS. PEARCE

Who shall I say is calling?

FREDDY

Freddy Eynsford Hill. If she doesn't remember me, tell
her I'm the chap who was sniggering at her.

MRS. PEARCE

(*Looking at him strangely*) Yes, sir.

FREDDY

And would you give her these? (*Hands her the nosegay*)

MRS. PEARCE

Yes, sir. (*She takes them and moves quickly to get the
door between her and this odd young man*)

FREDDY

You needn't rush. (*Gazing lovingly down the street*) I
want to drink in this street where she lives.

MRS. PEARCE

Yes, sir. (*She goes into the house*)

FREDDY

I have often walked down this street before;
But the pavement always stayed beneath my feet be-
fore.
All at once am I

Several stories high.
Knowing I'm on the street where you live.

Are there lilac trees in the heart of town?
Can you hear a lark in any other part of town?
Does enchantment pour
Out of ev'ry door?
No, it's just on the street where you live!

And oh! the towering feeling
Just to know somehow you are near!
The overpowering feeling
That any second you may suddenly appear!

People stop and stare. They don't bother me.
For there's nowhere else on earth that I would rather
    be.
Let the time go by,
I won't care if I
Can be here on the street where you live.
    (MRS. PEARCE *opens the door*)

MRS. PEARCE
(*Cautiously*) Mr. Eynsford-Hill?

FREDDY
Yes?

MRS. PEARCE
I'm terribly sorry, sir. Miss Doolittle says she doesn't
want to see anyone ever again.

FREDDY
But why? She was magnificent!

MRS. PEARCE
Magnificent? (*Not believing her ears*) Do you have the
right address, sir?

FREDDY
(*With calm resolution*) Of course. Tell her I'll wait.

MRS. PEARCE
But it might be days, sir. Even weeks!

FREDDY
But don't you see? I'll be happier here.
    (MRS. PEARCE *hastily goes back into the house*)

FREDDY

> People stop and stare. They don't bother me.
> For there's nowhere else on earth that I would rather
>> be.
> Let the time go by,
> I won't care if I
> Can be here on the street where you live.
>> (FREDDY *settles himself down on the doorstep for
>> the long wait*)

Scene 9

> HIGGINS' *study. There is a decanter of port and
> two glasses on the desk, next to them a carna-
> tion.*

TIME: *Evening. Six weeks later.*

AT RISE: HIGGINS, *in white tie, is pacing slowly up and
           down the room, thoughtfully detached.* PICKER-
           ING, *also formally dressed, is obviously nerv-
           ous.*

PICKERING

> Higgins, if there's any mishap at the Embassy tonight, if
> Miss Doolittle suffers any embarrassment whatever, it's
> on your head alone. I've been begging you to call off this
> experiment ever since Ascot.

HIGGINS

> (*Calmly*) Eliza can do anything. (*He continues his
> stroll*)

PICKERING

> But suppose she's discovered? Suppose she makes an-
> other ghastly mistake?

HIGGINS

> (*Good-humoredly*) There'll be no horses at the Ball,
> Pickering.

PICKERING

> (*In a panic*) But think how agonizing it would be! God,
> if anything happened tonight, I don't know what I'd do.

HIGGINS
(*Helpfully*) You could always rejoin your regiment.

PICKERING
(*Exploding*) Higgins, this is no time for flippancy. The way you've driven her these last six weeks has exceeded all the bounds of common . . . Oh, for God's sake, Higgins, stop pacing up and down! Can't you settle someplace?

HIGGINS
Have some port. It will quieten your nerves.

PICKERING
I'm not nervous! Where is it?

HIGGINS
On the desk.
     (PICKERING *goes to it and helps himself to a glass*)
     (MRS. PEARCE *comes out of the door on the landing*)

MRS. PEARCE
The car is here, sir.

HIGGINS
Thank you, Mrs. Pearce. Are you helping Eliza?

MRS. PEARCE
Yes, sir. (*She goes*)

PICKERING
Help her, indeed! I'll bet the damned gown doesn't fit. I warned you about those French designers. You should have gone to a good English store, where you knew everybody was on our side. Have a little port.

HIGGINS
No, thank you.

PICKERING
It will quieten your nerves.

HIGGINS
(*Still pacing*) No, thank you.

PICKERING
(*Exasperated*) Are you so sure she'll retain all you've hammered into her?

HIGGINS
We shall see.

PICKERING
But suppose she doesn't?

HIGGINS
Then I lose my bet. (*He settles himself comfortably on the sofa*)

PICKERING
(*Slightly irritated*) You know what I can't stand about you, Higgins? It's your confounded complacency. In a moment like this, with so much at stake, it's utterly indecent that you don't need a little port. What of the girl? You act as if she doesn't matter at all.

HIGGINS
Rubbish, Pickering. Of course she matters. What do you think I've been doing all these months? What could possibly matter more than to take a human being and change her into a different human being by creating a new speech for her? Why, it's filling up the deepest gulf that separates class from class, and soul from soul. She matters immensely.
(*ELIZA appears on the landing—a vision. She walks down the stairs and into the room.* HIGGINS *rises.* PICKERING *is overcome by her appearance.* HIGGINS *circles her inspecting her carefully*)

PICKERING
Miss Doolittle, you look beautiful.

ELIZA
Thank you, Colonel Pickering.

PICKERING
Don't you think so, Higgins?
(*ELIZA turns to* HIGGINS *hopefully*)

HIGGINS
(*Having decided the gown is quite all right*) Not bad. Not bad at all.
(*The* BUTLER *and* FOOTMAN *enter with coats, hats and* ELIZA'S *cape and help each into his.* HIGGINS *goes to the desk for his carnation which he slips into his buttonhole, then looking furtively around*)

to make certain PICKERING *doesn't see him, he
pours himself a quick glass of port. He starts briskly
for the door. At the threshold, he pauses, turns and
gazes at* ELIZA. *He returns to her and offers his arm.
She takes it and they go out the door,* PICKERING
following after)

Scene 10

> *The Promenade outside the ballroom of the
> Embassy.*

TIME: *Late that evening.*

AT RISE: *A* FOOTMAN *is on the landing announcing the
           guests as the names are given to him from a*
           FOOTMAN *above. The Promenade is filled with
           couples, some strolling on, some engaged in
           conversation with others.* MRS. HIGGINS *is
           chatting with friends.*

FOOTMAN
  Sir Reginald and Lady Tarrington.
        (SIR REGINALD *and* LADY TARRINGTON *descend the
        stairs and join friends in the room*)

FOOTMAN
  Professor Zoltan Karpathy.
        (KARPATHY *comes into the room. He is an im-
        portant-looking man with an astonishingly hairy
        face. He has an enormous mustache flowing out
        into luxuriant whiskers. His hair glows with oil.
        He is wearing several worthless orders. Obviously
        a foreigner, one would guess him as Hungarian in
        which case one would be right. In spite of the
        ferocity of his mustache, he is amiable and genially
        voluble. He joins some friends*)

FOOTMAN
  Colonel Hugh Pickering.
        (PICKERING *enters looking about for* MRS. HIGGINS.
        Seeing her, he goes to her)

PICKERING
  Mrs. Higgins!

MRS. HIGGINS
  (*To her group*) Excuse me. (*She and* PICKERING *separate themselves*)

PICKERING
  Well, she got by the first hurdle. (*With muffled excitement*) The Ambassador's wife was completely captivated.

MRS. HIGGINS
  I know. I've heard several people asking who she is. Do tell me what happened.

PICKERING
  Higgins said: "Madame Ambassador, may I introduce Miss Eliza Doolittle?" and Madame Ambassador said: "How do you do?" And Eliza came right back with: "How do you do?"

MRS. HIGGINS
  (*Disappointed*) Is that all?

PICKERING
  Oh, no! When it was my turn, both the Ambassador and his wife said to me: "Colonel Pickering, who is that captivating creature with Professor Higgins?"

MRS. HIGGINS
  What did you say?

PICKERING
  Well, I was stopped for a moment. Then I collected myself and I said: "Eliza Doolittle."

MRS. HIGGINS
  (*With sardonic appreciation*) That was very quick thinking, Colonel.

PICKERING
  (*Puffing up*) Thank you. Mrs. Higgins, do you think Eliza will make it?

MRS. HIGGINS
  Oh, I hope so! I've grown terribly fond of that girl.

FOOTMAN
Professor Henry Higgins.

(HIGGINS *appears on landing.* KARPATHY, *hearing his name, turns. As* HIGGINS *descends into the room,* KARPATHY *flings his arms wide apart and approaches him enthusiastically*)

KARPATHY
Ah, maestro! Maestro! (*He kisses* HIGGINS *on both cheeks*)

HIGGINS
(*Surprised, annoyed and wounded by the whiskers*) Oh! Oh!

KARPATHY
You remember me?

HIGGINS
No, I don't. Who the devil are you?

KARPATHY
I am your pupil, your first, best and greatest pupil. I am Zoltan Karpathy, that marvelous boy. I have made your name famous throughout Europe. You teach me phonetics. You cannot forget me.

HIGGINS
Why don't you shave?

KARPATHY
I have not your imposing appearance; your figure, your brow. Nobody notice me when I shave.

HIGGINS
(*Noticing his chest full of medals*) Where did you find all those old coins?

KARPATHY
(*Not at all offended—he can't be*) Decorations for language. The Queen of Transylvania is here this evening. I am indispensable to her at these international parties. I speak thirty-two languages. I know everybody in Europe. No imposter escape my detection. And now, Professor, you must introduce me to this glorious creature you escort this evening. She fascinate everyone. Not since Mrs. Langtry came to London . . .

FOOTMAN

His Excellency Dr. Themistocles Stephanos.
> (*A well-decorated gentleman and his lady descend the stairs and join a group*)

KARPATHY

(*Lowering his voice*) This so-called Greek diplomat pretends he cannot speak English. But he does not deceive me. He is the son of a Yorkshire watchmaker. He speaks English so villainously that he dare not utter a word of it without betraying his origin. I help him to pretend, but I make him pay through the nose. I make them all pay. (*He irritatingly strokes* HIGGINS' *lapel*) I look forward to meeting your lady. (*He bows, a bit too low, and rejoins his group*)
> (PICKERING, *who has overheard this conversation, is in a state when* HIGGINS *goes to him*)

PICKERING

Higgins, I say!

MRS. HIGGINS

(*Nervously*) Where's Eliza?

HIGGINS

Upstairs. Last minute adjustment.

PICKERING

I say, Higgins, let's not risk it. Let's collect her and leave immediately.

MRS. HIGGINS

Henry, do you think it wise to stay?

HIGGINS

Stay? Why not?

FOOTMAN

Miss Eliza Doolittle.
> (ELIZA *descends the stairs.* HIGGINS *crosses to join her at the foot. Everyone turns and everyone stares.* KARPATHY *immediately comes forward*)

KARPATHY

Ah, Professor, you must introduce me . . .
> (*He is interrupted by the strains of a regal march as the* QUEEN OF TRANSYLVANIA *and* CONSORT *make their grand entrance into the room. He re-*

treats and joins in the mass bowing. As the QUEEN
passes ELIZA *she is caught by her loveliness and
places her hand lightly on her cheek*)

QUEEN
   Charming. Charming.
      (*The* QUEEN *and* CONSORT *proceed to the ballroom
      as everyone rises to follow*)

Scene 11

      *The Ballroom of the Embassy. Sumptuous.
      Decorous.*

TIME: *Immediately following.*

Everyone has followed the QUEEN *into the ballroom. The waltz begins.* PROFESSOR KARPATHY
comes forward again and bows to HIGGINS, *in-
viting an introduction.* HIGGINS *bows cheerfully in
return, takes* ELIZA *in his arms and dances away
with her.*

KARPATHY, *now suspicious indeed, walks away.
Slowly, the ballroom fills with couples whirling
about in three-quarter time.* ELIZA *and* HIGGINS
dance off. Everyone changes partners and ELIZA
returns in the arms of another. KARPATHY *dances
his partner closer and closer to her. When partners
are changed again,* ELIZA *finds herself dancing with*
KARPATHY. *Inaudibly because of the music,* KAR-
PATHY *leads her into animated conversation; so
animated in fact, they stop dancing as the others
continue waltzing around them.*

PICKERING *enters and sees them. He frantically
waves across the room to attract* HIGGINS' *attention.* HIGGINS *comes forward.* PICKERING, *by
gestures, entreats* HIGGINS *to interrupt* KARPATHY
and ELIZA; *but* HIGGINS, *regarding this as the ulti-
mate test, decides to do nothing but watch and see
what will happen.*

The curtain descends slowly.

ACT TWO

Scene 1

HIGGINS' *study*.

TIME: *3:00 the following morning.*

AT RISE: *The* SERVANTS, *having tried to stay awake to learn the outcome of the ball, have lost their battle with sleep, and are in various positions of oblivion in the room. The clock strikes 3.* MRS. PEARCE *enters to awaken them as the sounds of voices are heard in the outside hall. They jump to their feet as* HIGGINS *and* PICKERING *enter.*

ELIZA follows. She is tired. Her expression is almost tragic. Seemingly unnoticed by all, she walks to the corner of the room and stands motionless by the desk as the two FOOTMEN *help* PICKERING *and* HIGGINS *off with their cloaks.*

PICKERING
(*Jubilant*) Higgins, it was an immense achievement.

HIGGINS
(*Yawning*) A silly notion. If I hadn't backed myself to do it, I should have chucked the whole thing up two months ago.

PICKERING
Absolutely fantastic.

HIGGINS
A lot of tomfoolery.

PICKERING
Higgins, I salute you.

HIGGINS

Nonsense, the silly people don't know their own silly business.

PICKERING

Tonight, old man, you did it!
You did it! You did it!
You said that you would do it,
And indeed you did.
I thought that you would rue it;
I doubted you'd do it.
But now I must admit it
That succeed you did.
You should get a medal
Or be even made a knight.

HIGGINS

It was nothing. Really nothing.

PICKERING

All alone you hurdled
Ev'ry obstacle in sight.

HIGGINS

Now, wait! Now, wait!
Give credit where it's due.
A lot of the glory goes to you.
(ELIZA *flinches violently but they take no notice of her. She recovers herself and stands stonily as before*)

PICKERING

But you're the one who did it,
Who did it, who did it!
As sturdy as Gibraltar,
Not a second did you falter.
There's no doubt about it,
You did it!
(*To* MRS. PEARCE)
I must have aged a year tonight.
At times I thought I'd die of fright.
Never was there a momentary lull.

HIGGINS

(*Lighting a cigar*)
Shortly after we came in

I saw at once we'd eas'ly win;
And after that I found it deadly dull.

PICKERING
(*To* MRS. PEARCE *and* MAIDS)
You should have heard the ooh's and ah's;
Ev'ry one wond'ring who she was.

HIGGINS
You'd think they'd never seen a lady before.

PICKERING
And when the Prince of Transylvania
Asked to meet her,
And gave his arm to lead her to the floor . . . !
(*To* HIGGINS)
I said to him: You did it!
You did it! You did it!
They thought she was ecstatic
And so damned aristocratic,
And they never knew
That you
Did it!
(ELIZA's *beauty becomes murderous*)

HIGGINS
Thank Heavens for Zoltan Karpathy. If it weren't for
him I would have died of boredom. He was there, all
right. And up to his old tricks.

MRS. PEARCE
Karpathy? That dreadful Hungarian? Was he there?

HIGGINS
Yes.

(*The* SERVANTS *gather around him, hanging on
every word*)
(*In his best dramatic manner*)
That blackguard who uses the science of speech
More to blackmail and swindle than teach;
He made it the devilish business of his
"To find out who this Miss Doolittle is."

Ev'ry time we looked around
There he was, that hairy hound
From Budapest.

Never leaving us alone,
Never have I ever known
A ruder pest.
Fin'lly I decided it was foolish
Not to let him have his chance with her.
So I stepped aside and let him dance with her.

Oozing charm from ev'ry pore,
He oiled his way around the floor.
Ev'ry trick that he could play,
He used to strip her mask away.
And when at last the dance was done
He glowed as if he knew he'd won!
And with a voice too eager,
And a smile too broad,
He announced to the hostess
That she was a fraud!

MRS. PEARCE
  No!

HIGGINS
  Yavol!

Her English is too good, he said,
Which clearly indicates that she is foreign.
Whereas others are instructed in their native language
English people aren.
And although she may have studied with an expert
Di'lectician and grammarian,
I can tell that she was born Hungarian!
      (*He and* PICKERING *roar with laughter*)
Not only Hungarian, but of royal blood, she is a prin-
cess!
      (*The* SERVANTS *can no longer contain their ad-
      miration*)

SERVANTS
  Congratulations, Professor Higgins,
  For your glorious victory!
  Congratulations, Professor Higgins!
  You'll be mentioned in history!
      (HIGGINS *accepts this spontaneous demonstration
      graciously. He seats himself on the sofa and
      modestly puffs his cigar*)

FOOTMAN	THE REST OF THE SERVANTS
This evening, sir, you did it!	Congratulations,
You did it! You did it!	Professor Higgins!
You said that you would do it!	For your glorious
And indeed you did.	Victory!
This evening, sir, you did it!	Congratulations,
You did it! You did it!	Professor Higgins!
We know that we have said it,	Sing a hail and halleluia
But—you did it and the credit	Ev'ry bit of credit
For it all belongs to you!	For it all belongs to you!

(PICKERING *joins in this final musical bravo*)

HIGGINS

(*Rising*) All I can say is, thank God it's all over. Now I can go to bed at last without dreading tomorrow.
(*The* SERVANTS *go off to bed*)

MRS. PEARCE

Good night, Mr. Higgins. (*She, too, goes*)

HIGGINS

Good night.

PICKERING

I think I shall turn in, too. It's been a great occasion. Goodnight, Higgins. (*He goes*)

HIGGINS

Goodnight, Pickering. Oh, Mrs. Pearce! (*But she is gone*) Oh damn, I meant to tell her I wanted coffee in the morning instead of tea. Leave a little for her, Eliza, will you? (*He looks around the room*) What the devil have I done with my slippers?

(*The slippers are by the desk.* ELIZA *tries to control herself, but no longer can. She hurls them at him with all her force*)

ELIZA

There are your slippers! And there! Take your slippers, and may you never have a day's luck with them!

HIGGINS

(*Astounded*) What on earth? (*He comes to her*) What's the matter? Is anything wrong?

ELIZA

(*Seething*) Nothing wrong—with you. I've won your

bet for you, haven't I? That's enough for you. I don't matter, I suppose?

HIGGINS

You won my bet! You! Presumptuous insect. *I* won it! What did you throw those slippers at me for?

ELIZA

Because I wanted to smash your face. I'd like to kill you, you selfish brute. Why didn't you leave me where you picked me out of—in the gutter? You thank God it's all over, and that now you can throw me back again there, do you?

HIGGINS

(*Looking at her in cool wonder*) So the creature is nervous, after all?

> (ELIZA *gives a suffocated scream of fury and instinctively darts her nails in his face.* HIGGINS *catches her wrists*)

Ah! Claws in you, you cat! How dare you show your temper to me? (*He throws her roughly onto the sofa*) Sit down and be quiet.

ELIZA

(*Crushed by superior strength and weight*) What's to become of me? What's to become of me?

HIGGINS

How the devil do I know what's to become of you? What does it matter what becomes of you?

ELIZA

You don't care. I know you don't care. You wouldn't care if I was dead. I'm nothing to you—not so much as them slippers.

HIGGINS

(*Thundering*) *Those* slippers.

ELIZA

(*With bitter submission*) Those slippers. I didn't think it made any difference now.

> (*A pause.* ELIZA *hopeless and crushed,* HIGGINS *a little uneasy*)

HIGGINS

(*In his loftiest manner*) Why have you suddenly begun

going on like this? May I ask whether you complain
of your treatment here?

ELIZA

No.

HIGGINS

Has anybody behaved badly to you? Colonel Pickering? Mrs. Pearce?

ELIZA

No.

HIGGINS

You don't pretend that I have treated you badly?

ELIZA

No.

HIGGINS

I'm glad to hear it. (*He moderates his tone*) Perhaps
you're tired after the strain of the day? (*He picks up a
box of chocolates*) Have a chocolate?

ELIZA

No. (*Recollecting her manners*) Thank you.

HIGGINS

(*Good-humored again*) I suppose it was natural for you
to be anxious, but it's all over now. (*He pats her kindly
on the shoulder. She writhes*) There's nothing more to
worry about.

ELIZA

No, nothing more for you to worry about. Oh God, I
wish I was dead.

HIGGINS

(*In sincere surprise*) Why, in Heaven's name, why?
Listen to me, Eliza. All this irritation is purely sub-
jective.

ELIZA

I don't understand. I'm too ignorant.

HIGGINS

It's only imagination. Nobody's hurting you. Nothing's
wrong. You go to bed like a good girl, and sleep it off.

Have a little cry and say your prayers; that will make you comfortable.

ELIZA

I heard your prayers. "Thank God it's all over!"

HIGGINS

(*Impatiently*) Well, don't you thank God it's all over? Now you are free and can do what you like.

ELIZA

(*Pulling herself together in desperation*) What am I fit for? What have you left me fit for? Where am I to go? What am I to do? What's to become of me?

HIGGINS

(*Enlightened, but not at all impressed*) Oh, that's what's worrying you, is it? (*Condescending to a trivial subject out of pure kindness*) Oh, I shouldn't bother about that if I were you. I should imagine you won't have much difficulty in settling yourself somewhere or other—though I hadn't quite realized you were going away. You might marry, you know. You see, Eliza, all men are not confirmed old bachelors like me and the Colonel. Most men are the marrying sort, poor devils. And you're not bad-looking. It's quite a pleasure to look at you at times. (*He looks at her*) Not now, of course. You've been crying and look like the very devil; but when you're all right and quite yourself, you're what I should call attractive. Come, you go to bed and have a good night's rest; and then get up and look at yourself in the glass; and you won't feel so cheap. (*Peering into the box of chocolates, in search of a creamy one. In the process, a genial afterthought occurs to him*) I daresay my mother could find some chap or other who would do very well.

ELIZA

We were above that in Covent Garden.

HIGGINS

What do you mean?

ELIZA

I sold flowers. I didn't sell myself. Now you've made a lady of me, I'm not fit to sell anything else.

HIGGINS

Tosh, Eliza, don't insult human relations by dragging all that cant about buying and selling into it. (*Not finding a creamy one, he puts the chocolates down*) You needn't marry the fellow if you don't want to.

ELIZA

What else am I to do?

HIGGINS

Oh, lots of things. What about that old idea of a florist's shop? Pickering could set you up in one. He's lots of money. (*Chuckling*) He'll have to pay for all those togs you've been wearing; and that, with the hire of the jewelry, will make a big hole in two hundred pounds. Oh, come! You'll be all right. I must clear off to bed; I'm devilish sleepy. By the way, I was looking for something. What was it?

ELIZA

Your slippers.

HIGGINS

Yes, of course. You shied them at me.
(*He picks them up and is starting for the stairs when she rises and speaks to him*)

ELIZA

Before you go, sir—

HIGGINS

(*Stopping, surprised at her calling him "sir"*) Eh?

ELIZA

Do my clothes belong to me or to Colonel Pickering?

HIGGINS

(*Coming back to her as if her question were the very climax of unreason*) What the devil use would they be to Pickering? Why need you start bothering about that in the middle of the night?

ELIZA

I want to know what I may take away with me. I don't want to be accused of stealing.

HIGGINS
(*Deeply wounded*) Stealing? You shouldn't have said that, Eliza. That shows a want of feeling.

ELIZA
I'm sorry. I'm only a common, ignorant girl; and in my station, I have to be careful. There can't be any feelings between the like of you and the like of me. Please will you tell me what belongs to me and what doesn't?

HIGGINS
(*Very sulky*) You may take the whole damned houseful if you like. Except the jewels. They're hired. Will that satisfy you? (*He turns on his heels and is about to go in extreme dudgeon*)

ELIZA
(*Drinking in his emotion like nectar and nagging him to provoke a further supply*) Stop, please! (*She takes off jewels*) Will you take these to your room and keep them safe? I don't want to run the risk of their being missing.

HIGGINS
(*Furious*) Hand them over!
      (*She gives him the jewels, he crams them into his pocket, unconsciously decorating himself with the protruding ends of the chains*)
If these belonged to me instead of the jeweler, I'd ram them down your ungrateful throat.

ELIZA
(*Taking a ring off*) This ring isn't the jeweler's; it's the one you bought me in Brighton. I don't want it now. (*He throws the ring violently across the room and turns on her so threateningly that she crouches with her hands over her face, and exclaims*) Don't you hit me.

HIGGINS
Hit you! You infamous creature, how dare you accuse me of such a thing? It is you who have hit me. You have wounded me to the heart.

ELIZA
(*Thrilling with hidden joy*) I'm glad. I've got a little of my own back, anyhow.

HIGGINS
(*With dignity, in his finest professional style*) You have

caused me to lose my temper, a thing that has hardly ever happened to me before. I prefer to say nothing more tonight. I am going to bed. (*He starts up the stairs*)

ELIZA

(*Pertly*) You'd better leave your own note for Mrs. Pearce about the coffee, for it won't be done by me!

HIGGINS

(*Stopping about halfway up the stairs*) Damn Mrs. Pearce! And damn the coffee! And damn you! And damn my own folly in having lavished my hard-earned knowledge and the treasure of my regard and intimacy on a heartless guttersnipe!

>(*He marches up the stairs with impressive decorum and spoils it by tripping on the top step. He successfully recovers but while looking to see if she noticed his awkwardness, he runs into the table and inadvertently turns on the machine. Guttural vowel sounds come pouring through the speaker. He turns it off violently and with a slam of the door, disappears.*) (ELIZA *runs to the ring on the floor and picks it up*)

ELIZA

>(*With smoldering fury*)
>Just you wait, Henry Higgins, just you wait!
>You'll be sorry but your tears'll be too late!
>You will be the one it's done to;
>And you'll have no one to run to;
>Just you wait, Henry Higgins, just you . . . .
>   (*She gives way to uncontrollable sobs*)

Scene 2

>*Outside* HIGGINS' *house.*

TIME: *Immediately following.*

AT RISE: FREDDY, *who has only left his post for changes of clothing, food and sleep, is seated on the doorstep.*

FREDDY
(Undaunted)

Are there lilac trees in the heart of town?
Can you hear a lark in any other part of town?
Does enchantment pour
Out of ev'ry door?
No, it's just on the street where you live!

And oh! the towering feeling
Just to know somehow she is near!
The overpowering feeling
That any second you may suddenly appear!
(ELIZA comes out of the house. She is wearing a daytime suit and is carrying a small suitcase. For the moment, FREDDY doesn't see her)
People stop and stare. They don't . . .
(He sees her now)
Darling!

ELIZA
(In a rage he does not understand) What are you doing here?

FREDDY
Nothing. I spend most of my time here. Oh, don't laugh at me, Miss Doolittle, but this is the only place . . .

ELIZA
(She puts down suitcase and grabs him by the shoulders)
Freddy, you don't think I'm a heartless guttersnipe, do you?

FREDDY
Oh, no, darling. How could you imagine such a thing? You know how I feel. I've written you two and three times a day telling you. Sheets and sheets . . .

Speak and the world is full of singing,
And I'm winging
Higher than the birds.
(In disgust, she turns away)
Touch and my heart begins to crumble,
The heavens tumble,
Darling, and I'm . . .

ELIZA
(Turning on him violently)

Words!
Words! Words! I'm so sick of words!
I get words all day through;
First from him, now from you!
Is that all you blighters can do?
   (FREDDY *is frightened*)

Don't talk of stars
Burning above;
If you're in love,
Show me!

Tell me no dreams
Filled with desire.
If you're on fire,
Show me!
   (*He opens his arms to show her and she pushes
   him away*)

Here we are together in the middle of the night!
Don't talk of spring! Just hold me tight!
Anyone who's ever been in love'll tell you that
This is no time for a chat!

Haven't your lips
Longed for my touch?
Don't say how much,
Show me! Show me!

Don't talk of love lasting through time.
Make me no undying vow.
Show me now!
   (*Bewildered but happy, he reaches for her again.
   She grabs his arm and fairly flings him down the
   street*)

Sing me no song!
Read me no rhyme!
Don't waste my time,
Show me!

Don't talk of June!
Don't talk of fall!
Don't talk at all!
Show me!

Never do I ever want to hear another word.

There isn't one I haven't heard.
Here we are together in what ought to be a dream;
Say one more word and I'll scream!

Haven't your arms
Hungered for mine?
Please don't "expl'ine,"
Show me! Show me!

Don't wait until wrinkles and lines
Pop out all over my brow,
Show me now!
> (*She picks up her suitcase and answers the longing look in his eyes by crowning him with it. Having released some of her anger against mankind in general, she marches off. He follows her, his arms out*)

FREDDY
> Darling . . . Darling . . . !

Scene 3

> Covent Garden. The Flower Market. A huge glass-enclosed market center. There is a public house just outside.

TIME: 5:00 that morning.

AT RISE: The market is coming to life. At first a few, then more and more vendors and flower girls walk on and prepare for business. A few COSTERMONGERS warm themselves around the smudge-pot fire. In the group are four who were warming themselves the night HIGGINS first met ELIZA. One of them starts whistling a few bars of the tune they sang. Three others pick it up.

MEN AT THE FIRE
> With one enormous chair . . .
> Oh, wouldn't it be loverly?

> Lots of choc'late for me to eat;

Lots of coal makin' lots of heat;
Warm face, warm hands, warm feet . . .
Oh, wouldn't it be loverly?

(ELIZA *walks into view and gazes around. She sees two flower girls she used to know and goes over to them. They jump to their feet as if they recognize her, then feel they've made a mistake and walk quickly away, one of them remarking that this "swell" looks very much like* ELIZA DOOLITTLE)

(ELIZA *sees the men at the fire and hesitantly walks toward them*)

Oh, so loverly sittin' absobloominlutely still!
I would never budge till spring
Crept over me winder sill.
Someone's head restin' on my knee;
Warm and tender as he can be,
Who takes good care of me.
Oh, wouldn't it be loverly . . . ?
Loverly! Loverly! . . .

(*They become aware of her presence, and their voices trail off. One of them rises*)

THAT ONE
Good morning, miss. Can I help you?

ELIZA
(*Looking hopefully into his face*) Do you mind if I warm my hands?

THAT ONE
Go right ahead, miss.

(*She kneels down to warm her hands. They all stare at her uncomfortably. One of them leans forward as if he knows her*)

ELIZA
Yes?

MAN LEANING FORWARD
(*Now leaning back*) Excuse me, miss. For a second there I thought you was somebody else.

ELIZA
Who?

SAME MAN
>Forgive me, ma'am. Early morning light playing tricks with me eyes.
>
>>(*He rises. They all do*)

IST MAN
>Can I get you a taxi, ma'am? A lady like you shouldn't be walkin' around London at this hour of the mornin'.

ELIZA
>(*Sadly*) No . . . thank you.

SAME MAN
>Good morning, miss.
>
>>(*They all move away from her, somewhat embarrassed. Two of them keep looking back, feeling that they know her from somewhere*)

ELIZA
>>(*More alone than she has ever been, picks up a bunch of violets from a basket next to the fire and stares at it*)
>
>Someone's head resting on my knee;
>Warm and tender as he can be,
>Who takes good care of me;
>Oh, wouldn't it be loverly . . . ?
>Loverly! Loverly!
>Loverly! Loverly!
>
>>(*She is interrupted by a loud commotion from the pub. HARRY enters. He is quite well-dressed. He is followed by the BARTENDER*)

HARRY
>Well, goodnight to you, Cecil. (*Calls into the pub*) Time to go, Alfie!
>
>>(*DOOLITTLE comes out of the pub. He is resplendently dressed as for a fashionable wedding and might be the bridegroom. A flower in his buttonhole, a dazzling silk hat and patent leather shoes complete the effect*)

BARTENDER
>Do come again, Mr. Doolittle. We value your patronage always.

DOOLITTLE
>(*Grandly*) Thank you, my good man. (*He gives him a*

generous tip) Here, take the missus a trip to Brighton.

BARTENDER

(*Gratefullly*) Thank you, Mr. Doolittle. (*He goes back into the Pub*)

ELIZA

(*Who has been watching, astounded*) Father!

DOOLITTLE

(*Seeing her*) You see, Harry, he has no mercy. Sent her down to spy on me in my misery, he did. Me own flesh and blood. (*He goes up to* ELIZA) Well, I'm miserable, all right. You can tell him that straight.

ELIZA

What are you talking about? What are you dressed up for?

DOOLITTLE

As if you didn't know! Go on back to that Wimpole Street devil and tell him what he done to me.

ELIZA

What has he done to you?

DOOLITTLE

He's ruined me, that's all. Destroyed me happiness. Tied me up and delivered me into the hands of middle-class morality. And don't you defend him. Was it him or was it not him that wrote to an old American blighter named Wallingford that was giving five millions to found moral reform societies, and tell him the most original moralist in England was Mr. Alfred P. Doolittle, a common dustman?

ELIZA

(*Bitterly*) That sounds like one of his jokes.

DOOLITTLE

You may call it a joke. It put the lid on me, right enough! The bloke died and left me four thousand pounds a year in his bloomin' will.

JAMIE

(*Coming out of the pub*) Oh, come on, Alfie. In a couple of hours you have to be at the church.

   (*A group of* DOOLITTLE'S *friends also emerge and motion him to come on back*)

ELIZA
  Church?

DOOLITTLE
  (*Tragically*) Yes, church. The deepest cut of all. Why
  do you think I'm dressed up like a ruddy pall-bearer?
  Your stepmother wants to marry me. Now I'm respectable—she wants to be respectable.

ELIZA
  If that's the way you feel, why don't you give the money
  back?

DOOLITTLE
  (*With melancholy resignation*) That's the tragedy of it,
  Eliza. It's easy to say chuck it, but I haven't the nerve.
  We're all intimidated. Intimidated, Eliza, that's what we
  are. And that's what I am. Bought up. That's what your
  precious professor has brought me to.

ELIZA
  Not my precious professor.

DOOLITTLE
  Oh, sent you back, has he? First he shoves me in the
  middle-class, then he chucks you out for me to support
  you. All part of his plan. (*Resourcefully*) But you
  double-cross him. Eliza. Don't you come home to me.
  Don't you take tuppence from me. You stand on your
  own two feet. You're a lady now and you can do it.
      (FREDDY *appears through the crowd*)

FREDDY
  Eliza, it's getting awfully cold in that taxi.

DOOLITTLE
  I say, you want to come and see me turned off this
  mornin'? St. George's, Hanover Square, ten o'clock.
  (*Sadly*) I wouldn't advise it, but you're welcome.

ELIZA
  No, thank you, Dad.

FREDDY
  (*To* ELIZA) Are you all finished here?

ELIZA
  (*With great finality*) Yes, Freddy. I'm all finished here.

(*She takes his arm*) Good luck, Dad.
> (*As a last gesture of farewell, she tosses away the violets and goes off with* FREDDY. DOOLITTLE *watches her go, rubbing his hands in satisfaction at having disposed of a knotty problem*)

JAMIE
Come along, Alfie.

DOOLITTLE
How much time do I have left?

JAMIE, HARRY AND FRIENDS
> There's just a few more hours.
> That's all the time you've got.
> A few more hours
> Before they tie the knot.
>> (DOOLITTLE *bows his head in despair*)

DOOLITTLE
There are drinks and girls all over London, and I have to track 'em down in just a few more hours.

> I'm getting married in the morning!
> Ding dong! The bells are gonna chime.
> Pull out the stopper!
> Let's have a whopper!
> But get me to the church on time!

> I gotta be there in the mornin'
> Spruced up and lookin' in me prime.
> Girls, come and kiss me;
> Show how you'll miss me.
> But get me to the church on time!

> If I am dancin'
> Roll up the floor.
> If I am whistlin'
> Whewt me out the door!

> For I'm gettin' married in the mornin'
> Ding dong! the bells are gonna chime.
> Kick up a rumpus
> But don't lose the compass;
> And get me to the church,
> Get me to the church,
> For Gawd's sake, get me to the church on time!

DOOLITTLE AND EVERYONE

I'm getting married in the morning
Ding dong! the bells are gonna chime.

DOOLITTLE

Drug me or jail me,
Stamp me and mail me.

ALL

But get me to the church on time!

I gotta be there in the morning
Spruced up and lookin' in me prime.

DOOLITTLE

Some bloke who's able
Lift up the table,

ALL

And get me to the church on time!

DOOLITTLE

If I am flying
Then shoot me down.
If I am wooin',
Get her out of town!

ALL

For I'm getting married in the morning!
Ding dong! the bells are gonna chime.

DOOLITTLE

Feather and tar me;
Call out the Army;
But get me to the church.

ALL

Get me to the church . . .

DOOLITTLE

For Gawd's sake, get me to the church on time! !
(*The* CROWD *pulls out the stopper and has a
whopper; a final street dance of farewell. When it's
over, dawn begins to make her presence known
through the glass roof.* DOOLITTLE'S *friends line up
to bid him a formal goodbye*)

HARRY AND EVERYONE

Starlight is reelin' home to bed now.

Mornin' is smearin' up the sky.
London is wakin'.
Daylight is breakin'.
Good luck, old chum,
Good health, goodbye.

DOOLITTLE
(*Solemnly shakes hand with all. In deepest gloom*)
I'm gettin' married in the mornin'
Ding dong! the bells are gonna chime . . .
Hail and salute me
Then haul off and boot me . . .
And get me to the church,
Get me to the church . . .
For Gawd's sake, get me to the church on time!
(DOOLITTLE *is lifted high in the air and carried off to the grim inevitable*)

Scene 4

The upstairs hall of HIGGINS' *house. There are three doors on the corridor and a telephone table and telephone.*

TIME: *Around 11:00, the following morning.*

AT RISE: HIGGINS *is bellowing from his room.*

HIGGINS
Pickering! Pickering!
(*He charges out of his room, followed by* MRS. PEARCE. *Having not finished dressing, he is wearing a dressing gown. He knocks violently on* PICKERING'S *door*)
Pickering! (*To* MRS. PEARCE) Didn't she say where to send her clothes?

MRS. PEARCE
I told you, sir, she took them all with her.

PICKERING
(*Entering; dressed*) What? What?

HIGGINS

Here's a confounded thing! ELIZA's bolted!

PICKERING

Bolted?

HIGGINS

Yes, bolted! And Mrs. Pearce let her go without telling me a word about it.

PICKERING

Well, I'm dashed!

HIGGINS

(*Pacing distractedly up and down*) What am I to do? I got tea this morning instead of coffee. I can't find anything. I don't know what appointments I've got.

MRS. PEARCE

Eliza would know.

HIGGINS

(*Rage and frustration*) Of course she would, but damn it she's gone.

MRS. PEARCE

Did either of you gentlemen frighten her last night?

PICKERING

You were there, Mrs. Pearce. We hardly said a word to her. (*Turning on* HIGGINS) Higgins, did you bully her after I went to bed?

HIGGINS

Just the other way around. She threw the slippers at me. I never gave her the slightest provocation. The slippers came bang at my head before I uttered a word. And she used the most perfectly awful language. I was shocked.

PICKERING

(*Stunned*) Well, I'm dashed.

HIGGINS

I don't understand it. She was shown every possible consideration. She admitted it herself.

PICKERING

(*Stunned*) Well, I'm dashed.

HIGGINS

(*Wildly*) Pickering, stop being dashed and do something.

PICKERING

What?

HIGGINS

Call the police! What are they there for, in Heaven's name? (*He starts into his room*)

MRS. PEARCE

(*Stopping him*) Mr. Higgins, you can't give Eliza's name to the police as if she were a thief, or a lost umbrella.

HIGGINS

Why not? I want to find her! The girl belongs to me! I paid five pounds for her! (*He charges into his room*)

PICKERING

Quite right. (*He picks up phone*) Scotland Yard, please. May I have some coffee, Mrs. Pearce?

MRS. PEARCE

Yes, sir. (*She goes*)

PICKERING

(*Sunnily, into phone*) Oh, good morning, old chap. Colonel Hugh Pickering, here . . . 27-A Wimpole Street. I want to report a missing person. Anything you can do to assist in her recovery will be frightfully appreciated. I'm not without influence, and I'll see to it that your superiors . . . Oh, yes. Eliza Doolittle . . . about twenty-one . . . I should say about five foot seven . . . Her eyes?

HIGGINS

(*Yelling from his room*) Brown!

PICKERING

(*Into the phone*) Brown . . . Her hair? Well, it's a rather neutral, nondescript color. I should say more on the . . .

HIGGINS

(*Bounding from his room*) Brown! Brown! Brown! (*Bounding back into his room*)

PICKERING

(*Into the phone*) Well, you heard what he said: brown

... Yes, this is her residence ... Between three and four
in the morning ... No ... No ... No ... No relation
at all. Let's just say a good friend. (*He laughs good-
humoredly*) Hmph? (*A troubled look clouds his face*)
Now, see here, my good man, I'm not at all pleased with
the tenor of that question. What the girl does here is our
affair. Your affair is to get her back so she can continue doing it! (*He hangs up furious with the inspector.*
HIGGINS *comes out of his room. He is now almost
dressed. Vexation knots his face*)

HIGGINS

What in all of Heaven could have prompted her to go?
After such a triumph at the ball?
What could have depressed her?
What could have possessed her?
I cannot understand the wretch at all!
    (*Shaking his head in exasperation, he goes back
    into his room to finish dressing*)

PICKERING

(*Who was only half listening, hits upon an idea. Calling
to* HIGGINS) Higgins, I have an old school chum at the
Home Office. Perhaps he can help. I'll call him. (*Picks
up phone*) Whitehall seven, two, double four, please.
(*He waits*)
    (HIGGINS *enters, struggling with his tie*)

HIGGINS

Women are irrational, that's all there is to that!
Their heads are full of cotton, hay, and rags!
They're nothing but exasperating, irritating,
Vacillating, calculating, agitating,
Maddening, and infuriating hags!
    (*He returns to his room*)

PICKERING

(*Into the phone*) Brewster Budgin, please ... Yes, I'll
wait! (*He waits*)
    (HIGGINS *enters*)

HIGGINS

Pickering, why can't a woman be more like a man?
    (PICKERING *looks at him, startled*)
Yes. Why can't a woman be more like a man?
Men are so honest, so thoroughly square;

Eternally noble, historically fair;
Who when you win will always give your back a pat.
Why can't a woman be like that?
Why does ev'ryone do what the others do?
Can't a woman learn to use her head?
Why do they do everything their mothers do?
Why don't they grow up like their father instead?
Why can't a woman take after a man?
Men are so pleasant, so easy to please;
Whenever you're with them, you're always at ease.
Would you be slighted if I didn't speak for hours?

PICKERING
Of course not.

HIGGINS
Would you be livid if I had a drink or two?

PICKERING
Nonsense.

HIGGINS
Would you be wounded if I never sent you flowers?

PICKERING
Never.

HIGGINS
Why can't a woman be like you?

One man in a million may shout a bit.
Now and then there's one with slight defects.
One perhaps whose truthfulness you doubt a bit.
But by and large we are a marvelous sex!

Why can't a woman behave like a man?
Men are so friendly, good-natured and kind;
A better companion you never will find.
If I were hours late for dinner, would you bellow?

PICKERING
Of course not.

HIGGINS
If I forgot your silly birthday, would you fuss?

PICKERING
Nonsense.

HIGGINS
    Would you complain if I took out another fellow?

PICKERING
  Never.

HIGGINS
    Why can't a woman be like us?
    (*Livid that they're not, he goes back into his room
    slamming the door behind him*)

PICKERING
  (*Into phone*) Hello, is Brewster Budgin there, please?
  (*Pause*) Boozy? You'll never, never, never guess who
  this is! (*Disappointed*) . . . Yes, it is. By George, what a
  memory! How are you, old fellow? It's so good to hear
  your voice again . . . Thirty years? It is really? Yes . . .
  oceans of water . . . yes . . . Boozy, old chap, I'll tell
  you why I called. Something rather unpleasant has happened at this end. Could I come right over and see you?
  Oh, good. I'll be right there. Thank you, Boozy. (*He
  hangs up as* MRS. PEARCE *enters with the coffee*) I'm
  going over to the Home Office, Mrs. Pearce.

MRS. PEARCE
  I do hope you find her, Colonel Pickering. Mr. Higgins
  will miss her.

PICKERING
  Mr. Higgins will miss her! Blast Mr. Higgins! I'll miss
  her! (*He goes*)
        (MRS. PEARCE *places the coffee on the table as*
        HIGGINS *comes out of his room, now fully dressed*)

HIGGINS
  Pickering! Pickering! (*He looks around*) Where's the
  Colonel?

MRS. PEARCE
  He's gone to the Home Office, sir.

HIGGINS
  Ah! You see, Mrs. Pearce? I'm disturbed and he runs to
  help. (*Touched*) Now there's a good fellow. Mrs.
  Pearce, you're a woman,

    Why can't a woman be more like a man?

Men are so decent, such regular chaps.
Ready to help you through any mishaps.
Ready to buck you up whenever you are glum.
Why can't a woman be a chum?

Why is thinking something women never do?
Why is logic never even tried?
Straightening up their hair is all they ever do.
Why don't they straighten up the mess that's inside?

Why can't a woman be more like a man?
If I were a woman who'd been to a ball,
Been hailed as a princess by one and by all;
Would I start weeping like a bathtub overflowing?
And carry on as if my home were in a tree?
Would I run off and never tell me where I'm going?
Why can't a woman be like me?
      (*He clamps his hat on his head and stalks off*)

Scene 5

> *The conservatory of* MRS. HIGGINS' *house.*

TIME: *Shortly after.*

AT RISE: MRS. HIGGINS *and* ELIZA *are having tea.*

MRS. HIGGINS
   And you mean to say that after you did this wonderful
   thing for them without making a single mistake, they just
   sat there and never said a word to you? Never petted
   you, or admired you, or told you how splendid you'd
   been?

ELIZA
   Not a word.

MRS. HIGGINS
   That's simply appalling. I should not have thrown the
   slippers at him, I should have thrown the fire irons.
      (ELIZA *smiles, but the smile is short-lived as* HIG-
      GINS *is heard thundering from the entrance hall*)

HIGGINS

(*Off*) Mother! Mother!
   (ELIZA *looks fearful and rises to leave*)

MRS. HIGGINS

(*Staying her*) I thought it wouldn't be long. Stay where you are, my dear.

HIGGINS

(*Off*) Mother, where the devil are you?

MRS. HIGGINS

Remember, last night you not only danced with a prince, but you behaved like a princess.
   (ELIZA *collects herself as* HIGGINS *charges into the room*)

HIGGINS

Mother, the damndest . . . ! (*He sees* ELIZA. *Amazed. Angry*) You!

ELIZA

(*Giving a staggering exhibition of ease of manner*) How do you do, Professor Higgins? Are you quite well?

HIGGINS

(*Choking*) Am I . . . (*He can say no more*)

ELIZA

But of course you are. You are never ill. Would you care for some tea?

HIGGINS

Don't you dare try that game on me! I taught it to you! Get up and come home and don't be a fool! You've caused me enough trouble for one morning!

MRS. HIGGINS

Very nicely put, indeed, Henry. No woman could resist such an invitation.

HIGGINS

How did this baggage get here in the first place?

MRS. HIGGINS

Eliza came to see me, and I was delighted to have her. And if you don't promise to behave yourself, I shall have to ask you to leave.

HIGGINS

You mean I'm to put on my Sunday manners for this thing I created out of the squashed cabbage leaves of Covent Garden?

MRS. HIGGINS

(*Calmly*) Yes, dear, that is precisely what I mean.

HIGGINS

I'll see her damned first! (*He walks to the rear of the conservatory and paces back and forth noisily*)

MRS. HIGGINS

(*To* ELIZA) How did you ever learn manners with my son around?

ELIZA

(*Sweetly, but making certain her voice carries*) It was very difficult. I should never have known how ladies and gentlemen behave if it hadn't been for Colonel Pickering. He always showed me that he felt and thought about me as if I were something better than a common flower girl. You see, Mrs. Higgins, apart from the things one can pick up, the difference between a lady and a flower girl is not how she behaves, but how she is treated. I shall always be a flower girl to Professor Higgins because he always treats me as a flower girl and always will. But I know that I shall always be a lady to Colonel Pickering because he always treats me as a lady, and always will.

(*There is a strange gnashing noise from the rear of the conservatory*)

MRS. HIGGINS

Henry, please don't grind your teeth.

(*The* PARLOR MAID *enters*)

MAID

The Vicar is here, madam. Shall I show him into the garden?

MRS. HIGGINS

(*Horrified*) The Vicar, and the Professor? Good Heavens, no! I'll see him in the library.

(*The* MAID *goes.* MRS. HIGGINS *rises to follow*)

Eliza, if my son begins to break things, I give you full permission to have him evicted. (*At the door, she turns back to* HIGGINS) Henry, dear, if I were you, I should stick to two subjects, the weather and your health. (*She goes*)

(HIGGINS *comes down to the tea table. He looks at* ELIZA *quizzically; while deciding on a method of attack he pours himself some tea. He decides on restraint*)

HIGGINS

Well, Eliza, you've had a bit of your own back, as you call it. Have you had enough? And are you going to be reasonable? Or do you want any more?

ELIZA

You want me back only to pick up your slippers and put up with your tempers and fetch and carry for you.

HIGGINS

I haven't said I wanted you back at all.

ELIZA

(*Turns to him*) Oh, indeed. Then what are we talking about?

HIGGINS

About you, not about me. If you come back I shall treat you just as I have always treated you. I can't change my nature; and I don't intend to change my manners. My manners are exactly the same as Colonel Pickering's.

ELIZA

That's not true. He treats a flower girl as if she was a duchess.

HIGGINS

And I treat a duchess as if she was a flower girl.

ELIZA

Oh, I see. (*She rises composedly and walks away*) The same to everybody.

HIGGINS

Just so. (*He sits at the table*) ... The great secret, Eliza, is not having bad manners or good manners or any other particular sort of manners, but having the same manner for all human souls. The question is not whether I treat you rudely, but whether you ever heard me treat anyone else better.

ELIZA

(*With sudden sincerity*) I don't care how you treat me. I don't mind your swearing at me. I shouldn't mind a black eye: I've had one before this. But I won't be passed over.

HIGGINS

Then get out of my way: for I won't stop for you. You talk about me as if I were a motor bus.

ELIZA

So you are a motor bus: all bounce and go, and no consideration for anyone. But I can get along without you. Don't think I can't.

HIGGINS

I know you can. I told you you could. (*Pause, seriously*) You never wondered, I suppose, whether I could get along without you.

ELIZA

Don't try to get around me. You'll have to.

HIGGINS

(*Arrogantly*) And so I can. Without you or any soul on earth. (*With sudden humility*) But I shall miss you, Eliza. I've learned something from your idiotic notions. I confess that humbly and gratefully.

ELIZA

Well, you have my voice on your gramophone. When you feel lonely without me you can turn it on. It's got no feelings to hurt.

HIGGINS

I can't turn your soul on.

ELIZA

Oh, you are a devil. You can twist the heart in a girl as easily as some can twist her arms to hurt her. What am I to come back for?

HIGGINS

(*Heartily*) For the fun of it. That's why I took you on.

ELIZA

And you may throw me out tomorrow if I don't do everything you want me to?

HIGGINS

Yes: and you may walk out tomorrow if I don't do everything you want me to.

ELIZA

And live with my father?

HIGGINS

Yes, or sell flowers. Or would you rather marry Pickering?

ELIZA

(*Fiercely*) I woudn't marry you if you asked me; and you're nearer my age than what he is.

HIGGINS

(*Correcting her gently*) Than he is.

ELIZA

(*Losing her temper and walking away from him*) I'll talk as I like. You're not my teacher now. That's not what I want and don't you think it. I've always had chaps enough wanting me that way. Freddy Hill writes to me twice and three times a day, sheets and sheets.

HIGGINS

(*Coming to her*) Oh, in short, you want me to be as infatuated about you as he is. Is that it?

ELIZA

(*Facing him, much troubled*) No, I don't. That's not the sort of feeling I want from you. I want a little kindness. I know I'm a common ignorant girl, and you a book-learned gentleman; but I'm not dirt under your feet. What I done—(*Correcting herself*) What I did was not for the dresses and the taxis: I did it because we were pleasant together and I come—came to care for you; not to want you to make love to me, and not forgetting the difference between us, but more friendly like.

HIGGINS

Yes, of course. That's just how I feel. And how Pickering feels. Eliza, you're a fool.

ELIZA

That's not a proper answer to give me.

HIGGINS

It's all you'll get until you stop being a plain idiot. If you're going to be a lady you'll have to stop feeling neglected if the men you know don't spend half their time sniveling over you and the other half giving you black eyes. You find me cold, unfeeling, selfish, don't you? Very well: Be off with you to the sort of people you like. Marry some sentimental hog or other with lots of money, and a thick pair of lips to kiss you with and a thick pair of boots to kick you with. If you can't appreciate what you've got, you'd better get what you can appreciate.

ELIZA

(*Desperate*) I can't talk to you: you turn everything against me. I'm always in the wrong. But don't you be too sure that you have me under your feet to be trampled on and talked down. I'll marry Freddy, I will, as soon as I'm able to support him.

HIGGINS

(*Disagreeably surprised*) Freddy!! That poor devil who couldn't get a job as an errand boy even if he had the guts to try for it! Woman, do you not understand? I have made you a consort for a king!

ELIZA

Freddy loves me: that makes him king enough for me. I don't want him to work: he wasn't brought up to it as I was. (*Determinedly*) I'll go and be a teacher.

HIGGINS

What'll you teach, in heaven's name?

ELIZA

What you taught me. I'll teach phonetics.

HIGGINS

Ha! Ha! Ha!

ELIZA

I'll offer myself as an assistant to that brilliant Hungarian!

HIGGINS

(*In a fury*) What! That imposter! That humbug! That toadying ignoramus! Teach him my methods! My dis-

coveries? (*He strides toward her*) You take one step in
that direction and I'll wring your neck. Do you hear?

ELIZA

(*Defiantly nonresistant*) Wring away! What do I care?
I knew you'd strike me one day. (HIGGINS, *about to lay
hands on her, recoils*) Aha! That's done you, 'enry
'iggins, it 'as. Now I don't care that—(*she snaps her
fingers in his face*) for your bullying and your big talk.

What a fool I was! What a dominated fool!
To think you were the earth and sky.
What a fool I was! What an addle-pated fool!
What a mutton-headed dolt was I!
No, my reverberating friend,
You are not the beginning and the end!

HIGGINS

(*Wondering at her*) You impudent hussy! There isn't
an idea in your head or a word in your mouth that I
haven't put there.

ELIZA

There'll be spring ev'ry year without you.
England still will be here without you.
There'll be fruit on the tree,
And a shore by the sea;
There'll be crumpets and tea
Without you.

Art and music will thrive without you.
Somehow Keats will survive without you.
And there still will be rain
On that plain down in Spain,
Even that will remain
Without you.
I can do
Without you.

You, dear friend, who talk so well,
You can go to Hertford, Hereford and Hampshire!

They can still rule the land without you.
Windsor Castle will stand without you.
And without much ado
We can all muddle through
Without you!

HIGGINS

(*Fascinated*) You brazen hussy!

ELIZA

Without your pulling it, the tide comes in,
Without your twirling it, the earth can spin.
Without your pushing them, the clouds roll by.
If they can do without you, ducky, so can I!

I shall not feel alone without you.
I can stand on my own without you.
So go back in your shell,
I can do bloody well
Without . . .

HIGGINS

(*Triumphantly*)
By George, I really did it!
I did it! I did it!
I said I'd make a woman
And indeed I did!

I knew that I could do it!
I knew it! I knew it!
I said I'd make a woman
And succeed I did!

Eliza, you're magnificent! Five minutes ago you were a
millstone around my neck. Now you're a tower of
strength, a consort battleship! I like you like this!
    (ELIZA *stares at him stonily, then turns on her heels
    and walks to the door*)

ELIZA

(*Quietly at the door*) Good-bye, Professor Higgins. I
shall not be seeing you again. (*She goes*)
    (HIGGINS *is thunderstruck. He walks falteringly
    across the room and looks after her*)

HIGGINS

(*Calling for help*) Mother! Mother!
    (MRS. HIGGINS *enters*)

MRS. HIGGINS

What is it, Henry? What has happened?

HIGGINS

(*More to himself*) She's gone!

MRS. HIGGINS
(*Gently*) Of course, dear. What did you expect?

HIGGINS
(*Bewildered*) What am I to do?

MRS. HIGGINS
Do without, I suppose.

HIGGINS
(*With sudden defiance*) And so I shall! If the Higgins
oxygen burns up her little lungs, let her seek some
stuffiness that suits her. She's an owl sickened by a few
days of my sunshine! Very well, let her go! I can do
without her! I can do without anybody! I have my own
soul! My own spark of divine fire! (*He marches off*)

MRS. HIGGINS
(*Applauding*) Bravo, Eliza! (*She smiles*)

Scene 6

Outside HIGGINS' *house, Wimpole Street.*

TIME: *Dusk, that afternoon.*

AT RISE: HIGGINS *enters bellowing with rage.*

HIGGINS
Damn!! Damn!! Damn!! Damn!! (*A sudden terrifying
discovery*) I've grown accustomed to her face!
   She almost makes the day begin.
   I've grown accustomed to the tune
   She whistles night and noon.
   Her smiles. Her frowns.
   Her ups, her downs,
   Are second nature to me now;
   Like breathing out and breathing in.
      (*Reassuringly*)
   I was serenely independent and content before we met;
   Surely I could always be that way again—
      (*The reassurance fails*)
                                          and yet

I've grown accustomed to her looks;
Accustomed to her voice:
Accustomed to her face.

(*Bitterly*) Marry Freddy! What an infantile idea! What
a heartless, wicked, brainless thing to do! But she'll regret it! She'll regret it. It's doomed before they even take
the vow!

I can see her now:
Mrs. Freddy Eynsford-Hill,
In a wretched little flat above a store.

I can see her now:
Not a penny in the till,
And a bill-collector beating at the door.

She'll try to teach the things I taught her,
And end up selling flow'rs instead;
Begging for her bread and water,
While her husband has his breakfast in bed!

(*Fiendishly pleased*)
In a year or so
When she's prematurely gray,
And the blossoms in her cheek has turned to chalk,

She'll come home and lo!
He'll have upped and run away
With a social climbing heiress from New York!

(*Tragically*)
Poor Eliza!
How simply frightful!
How humiliating!
    (*Irresistibly*)
How delightful!
    (*He walks to his door*)

How poignant it will be on that inevitable night when she
hammers on my door in tears and rags. Miserable and
lonely, repentant and contrite. Will I let her in or hurl
her to the wolves? Give her kindness, or the treatment
she deserves? Will I take her back, or throw the baggage
out?

(*With sudden benevolence*)

I'm a most forgiving man;
The sort who never could,
Ever would,
Take a position and staunchly never budge.
Just a most forgiving man.

(*With sudden vindictiveness*)
But I shall never take her back,
If she were crawling on her knees.
Let her promise to atone!
Let her shiver, let her moan!
I will slam the door and let the hell-cat freeze!

Marry Freddy! Ha!
(*He takes out his keys to open the door but stops in despair*)

But I'm so used to hear her say:
Good morning every day.
Her joys, her woes,
Her highs, her lows
Are second nature to me now;
Like breathing out and breathing in.
I'm very grateful she's a woman
And so easy to forget;
Rather like a habit
One can always break—and yet
I've grown accustomed to the trace
Of something in the air;
Accustomed to her face.

Scene 7

HIGGINS' *study.*

TIME: *Immediately following.*

AT RISE: *The blue-gray light of early evening pours in
          through the window. Only one or two lamps
          are on.*

          HIGGINS *walks into the room. He walks around
          thoughtfully. He comes to the xylophone and*

picks up the mallet and looks at it for a moment. He slowly walks over to the machine by the door and turns it on. ELIZA's voice is heard on the speaker. He goes back to his desk and decides to sit on the stool rather than his own chair behind the desk. His hat still on, his head bowed, he listens to the recording.

ELIZA'S VOICE

I want to be a lady in a flower shop instead of selling flowers at the corner of Tottenham Court Road. But they won't take me unless I talk more genteel. He said he could teach me. Well, here I am ready to pay, not asking any favor—and he treats me as if I was dirt. I know what lessons cost, and I'm ready to pay.

    (ELIZA *walks softly into the room and stands for a moment by the machine looking at* HIGGINS)

HIGGINS' VOICE

It's almost irresistible. She's so deliciously low, so horribly dirty. (ELIZA *turns off the machine*)

ELIZA

(*Gently*) I washed my face and hands before I come, I did.

    (HIGGINS *straightens up. If he could but let himself, his face would radiate unmistakable relief and joy. If he could but let himself, he would run to her. Instead, he leans back with a contented sigh pushing his hat forward till it almost covers his face*)

HIGGINS

(*Softly*) Eliza? Where the devil are my slippers?

    (*There are tears in* ELIZA's *eyes. She understands*)
        The curtain falls slowly